Endorsements

Referrals are the holy grail in real estate. All real estate agents want them, but few know how to generate them in a consistent, steady way because the old-age advice for referrals is to ask for them. But Stacey shows you how to unleash a referral explosion by turning your referral strategy on its head. Do yourself a favor and read this book. To be one of the best real estate agents you need to master generating referrals without asking for them. You will also learn the steps on how to build a referral generation plan that you can follow for years to come, bringing in more referrals than you can imagine.

Pat Hiban, *New York Times* Best Selling Author of
*6 steps to 7 Figures: A Real Estate Professional's Guide to
Building Wealth and Creating Your Destiny.* Chairman of
the Board of Rebus University,
Podcast Host of Real Estate Rockstars

Stacey Brown Randall gets it! She has been there, done that and got the tee-shirt. In this day and age when we are all actually in sales, Stacey has assembled a masterpiece that has you focus on what you do best—deliver and with the structure and systems she provides for you in this book, business just naturally flows.

Chris Spurvey, author of *It's Time to Sell:
Cultivating the Sales Mind-Set.* Former VP of Business
>ment of Atlantic Canada, KPMG

What am I doing up in the middle of the night reading this book when I should be sleeping? Finally solving the referral marketing challenge. I know referrals are important for growing my law firm and I even had a few of the pieces of the process in place to get referrals. But I hadn't put it all together...until Stacey Brown Randall's book came along. Stacey's book defines and helps you construct the entire referral system end-to-end. And guess what? It isn't difficult. In many ways it's common sense. But Stacey's beautiful way of dispelling myths, previous beliefs and refocusing you on what is important to nurture referral relationships has finally lifted the fog for me. I am so grateful for this book.

Neil W. Tyra, Esq., The Tyra Law Firm, LLC. Host of *"The Law Entrepreneur"* Podcast

Stacey Brown Randall gets it right with her book, *Generating Business Referrals Without Asking*. In a category where many books address tricks of the trade, or repeat flawed ideas, Stacey delivers a refreshing and authentic look at how to be referable, and how to change your mindset as someone who gets referred for their clients' reasons, not because they think they are owed referrals. Read this book and implement Stacey's advice to find yourself getting referrals to grow your business.

Timothy Flanagan, CLU, ChFC, CFP, ChSNC.
President, Mass Mutual Carolinas

Everybody in sales knows that qualified and motivated referrals are the key to business growth. *Generating Business Referrals Without Asking* outlines the misconceptions and dead ends that constitute most of today's "best advice." Stacey's clear, creative and compelling stories shows the path to real referral success. This book is a must read for anybody who wants to power their business through high octane referrals.

Ken Samuelson, Principle, The Morehead Group

After being an entrepreneur for 17 years and working in one of the most competitive industries, referrals are still the best way to attract, maintain and grow a company's sales and revenues. *Generating Business Referrals Without Asking* helps even the most experienced and seasoned professionals find gaps in their presentation and personal style in driving more business. The methodology is a fresh approach on a wonderful strategy to exponentially grow your business and income. The best thing about this book may just be that it will help you enrich your professional relationships and help create a continued fulfilling career.

Jeff Douglas, CEO, Wyndham Capital Mortgage, Inc.
"The Nation's Most Referable Lender"™

A quick and powerful read packed full of value. We all need to grow our business and there is ONE approach that has been key to building three successful companies—referrals from people that know, like and trust you. *Generating Business Referrals Without Asking* is clearly written, well organized and most importantly gives you the exact blueprint to create a steady stream of qualified referrals. Thank you for writing this Stacey. This is a gift, and a must read, for businesses of any size!

John Ramstead, Certified Leadership Coach, Beyond Influence, LLC. Host of Eternal Leadership Podcast

Stacey has developed a well-thought out process that when followed consistently delivers results. After putting into practice Stacey's principles for attracting referrals, I can tell you simply that it works. The very best part is the process allows me to be genuine in thanking people who have referred my business. Wish I had read this book 20 years ago but the major changes to my referral strategy leave my business well poised for the next 20 years.

Michelle O'Connor, O'Connor Insurance & Associates

Stacey has not only hit the nail on the head about why we don't like to ask for referrals, but has explained to us why they don't work, allowing us to no longer feel guilty about not following supposedly the oldest and best practices of all the selling gurus. And she goes even further to give us strategies and a plan to implement that will ensure we obtain and grow our referral base, in a very comfortable, easy way. Last, but not least, if her strategies and plan aren't working, she dares to talk about the why—us—and how to correct those issues.

Brandy Milazzo, Managing Partner,
Milazzo Webb Law, PLLC

In *Generating Business Referrals Without Asking*, Stacey outlines easy to follow strategies that have made a tremendous impact on my business. Prior to Stacey, I had been pushing for names and introductions then I was left wondering why the sales process took so long to develop. Now I use Stacey's techniques to create a positive environment that encourages referrals from my most trusted Centers of Influence. When I receive a quality referral, trust in me is transferred from the referral source to the potential client cutting the getting-to-know you process from months to days... I sincerely appreciate Stacey and will keep this book close at hand.

Frank Goins, CFP, CTFA,
Wealth Advisor, SunTrust Bank

Stacey Brown Randall answers the questions about 'Generating Business Referrals' in this remarkable book! She weaves together her research, business tools and applications into a book that helps solve the challenge of growing one's business through actual referrals. As a terrific story teller, Stacey shares anecdotes from her business as well as successes she has helped cultivate in her clients. It is a book that is a great read as well as one that can be referenced as one implements her brilliant strategies. A terrific addition to any professional business library!

Ellen Linares, CLTC, CLU, ChFC,
Financial Advisor, HF Financial

In Generating Business Referrals Without Asking, Stacey gives entrepreneurs a roadmap to building sustainable business through authenticity that taps into our most genuine and positive human traits as human. Stacey's book is a must-read for anyone who's ever been annoyed by the "What can I do to put you in this used car today?' ethos of traditional sales and business development.

Tim Whitmire, Co-Founder of F3 Nation
and The Iron Project

GENERATING BUSINESS REFERRALS
WITHOUT ASKING

GENERATING BUSINESS
REFERRALS
Without Asking

A SIMPLE
5 STEP
PLAN TO A
REFERRAL
EXPLOSION

STACEY BROWN RANDALL

NEW YORK

LONDON • NASHVILLE • MELBOURNE • VANCOUVER

Generating Business Referrals Without Asking

A Simple 5 Step Plan to a Referral Explosion

© 2019 Stacey Brown Randall

Published in New York, New York, by Morgan James Publishing. Morgan James is a trademark of Morgan James, LLC. www.MorganJamesPublishing.com

The Morgan James Speakers Group can bring authors to your live event. For more information or to book an event visit The Morgan James Speakers Group at www.TheMorganJamesSpeakersGroup.com.

ISBN 9781683509264 paperback
ISBN 9781683509271 eBook
Library of Congress Control Number: 2018930151

Interior Design by:
Chris Treccani
www.3dogcreative.net

In an effort to support local communities, raise awareness and funds, Morgan James Publishing donates a percentage of all book sales for the life of each book to Habitat for Humanity Peninsula and Greater Williamsburg.

Get involved today! Visit
www.MorganJamesBuilds.com

Dedication

To all those who refuse to ask for referrals.
You were right all along.

To my father, Steve Brown,
the real writer of our family and our first published
author. I am a strong woman today because I have a
strong father who always believes in me.

Acknowledgements

Writing a book is a labor of love, takes a lot of time and needs a tribe to make it happen (especially on deadline).

To my editor, Susan Snowden who continues the tradition of editing the Brown family authors—thank you for your guidance and your willingness to stock up on red pens. I'm pretty confident you used at least a dozen through our many editing rounds.

To the publishing team at Morgan James Publishing, thank you for welcoming me into the world of publishing and for your guidance throughout the journey. I appreciate your desire to make sure we had a book we could both be proud of.

To Tom Schwab of Interview Valet, where a chance meeting at a conference led to keeping in touch and then you referring me to David Hancock, the CEO of Morgan James Publishing. You knocked over the first domino in this journey to see this book in print.

To my friends who always encourage me…Brandy, Arden, Ellen, Danielle, Rebecca and many others, too many to name, thank you for your encouragement. I am lucky to have women in my life who share in my accomplishments and are never threatened by them.

To my parents, Steve and Mary Ella, who gave me two precious gifts that I am incredibly grateful for. The gift of confidence and the love of reading…I'm pretty sure my ability to write started when you instilled in me the joy that came from reading. Amazing how those extra 30 minutes past bedtime dedicated to just reading can jump start a child's desire to read more.

To my children, Jacob, Dani and McKenzie. I am keenly aware that my work and my writing take me away from you. But your love, encouragement and willingness to share me with the work I love are the greatest gifts you can give me. May you always be willing to go after what you want in life and have a tribe to support you along the way. Your dad and I could not be prouder or amazed at who you are becoming.

To my husband, Norm. When I needed time away to write, you said go. When I needed extra time away to write, you said stay longer. When I needed a Coca-Cola to get through, you delivered. When I needed encouragement, you were there. When I needed to be reminded why I would put myself through the process of writing a book, you always found the right words. The greatest gift you give me is your faith in me and I am extremely grateful that my success is our success and you want great things for me.

And to those first few clients who asked to learn my referral generating process which allowed me to figure out it was just five simple steps that I could teach to others…you made all of this possible. You were there when I built my online program

Growth By Referrals, you were there as I wrote each page of this book and you are there each time someone learns the simple process to generate referrals without asking. Your curiosity changed my life.

Table of Contents

A DIFFERENT REFERRAL PHILOSOPHY

Many receive advice, only the wise profit from it.
Harper Lee, author of *To Kill a Mockingbird*

E very expert or guru out there teaches what they know, supposedly (wink, wink).

They form a philosophy that is at the center of what they believe. And their philosophy informs the strategies and processes they teach you. From those strategies and processes come the tactics and tools they believe you need to use to be successful. So when you decide to listen to experts or gurus make sure you understand their philosophy first. It allows you to be a better consumer of their message and materials.

I am no different. Though a contrarian when it comes to the general and decades-old advice you have been hearing about how to generate referrals, which has always been "just ask," I offer tactics, tools, and processes you'll need to follow to generate referrals *without* asking. Whether this is your tenth year in business or your first ten months, generating referrals should be a business development strategy you master if you want to make the continual growth of your business easier for you. Which takes us to our first stop on this journey to understanding my philosophy on generating referrals and specifically generating referrals without asking.

My referral philosophy is:

Referrals come from relationships.

And relationships come from connections.

And connections are built through ongoing touch points.

Think of it this way…

REFERRALS

TOUCH POINTS   RELATIONSHIPS

CONNECTIONS

The philosophy is simple, nothing rocket science about it, but everything I teach starts and ends with this philosophy. I believe it is the only truth that matters when you want to generate referrals without asking. You need to build relationships and to do that you need to be investing in and connecting with the people you want to receive referrals from. The best way to connect and strengthen those relationships is through ongoing touch points. Touch points are just the outreach you do to connect. We'll dive more into the types of touch points (what works, what doesn't) later on but it's important for you to understand that ongoing touch points go deeper than just "keeping in touch." Keeping-in-touch outreach is like a quick "check-in" email or a quick "how are you?" phone call. The touch points I will teach you elevate you past keeping in touch and move you to staying top of mind.

I believe you cannot violate this philosophy when it comes to generating referrals, especially if you want to have any level of long-term sustainability. My philosophy stems from understanding the true definition of a referral. A referral is a connection made by a trusted friend, peer or colleague to connect one person who has a problem or a need to the person who can solve that problem or meet the need. Following this definition of a referral and my philosophy, I have been able to generate triple digit (100+) referrals year after year. My clients have had the same success as well.

I can't promise that just reading this book will instantly double, triple or quadruple your referral success in a matter of moments (or even months). That's the stuff of get-rich-quick schemes and late-night infomercials. There is work involved. No way around it.

But I have found generating new clients through referrals to be hands down the easiest way to grow my business. Yes, there is work involved—a process you need to follow consistently—but I'd rather do my "referral work" over cold calling, incessant networking or stalking people on social media any day of the week. This is especially true the longer you have been in business. We have a tendency to fall into ruts to grow our businesses and those ruts can hold us back from truly experiencing easier growth. Or we fall victim to chasing the latest and greatest sales tactic, where we spend a lot of time and energy but don't always get the results we desire.

Consider a client of mine, Gray Langley, the managing partner of a CPA firm. He has been a CPA for over thirty years and has been serving as the managing partner since 1999. His firm has grown incrementally over time and, overall, he was satisfied with the growth. But then he was introduced to my program through a friend. Here is what Gray shared about the value of being open to a perspective you may not have previously considered.

> … *before I learned about Stacey's Growth by Referrals Program, I'd been filling the managing partner role for 18 years with the responsibility of bringing in new clients. I had good success, and I was happy with the success. But then, something was gnawing at me because I thought as good as I'm doing, or as I think I'm doing, could I do better? An individual in another field said, oh this woman's program really changed how I look at my business, and I*

thought, well, why am I so stubborn that I think that I am the only person that has the answers that can chart the direction that I want the growth of our firm to go? Maybe it would be a good idea to just have someone look over my shoulder and help me realize that I don't have all the answers and that I can probably improve upon how I do things if I'll ask for help. No one likes to admit that they need to help, but it's something that we all need at some point in our lives.

To increase your referral success, you need to be prepared to shift your thinking. And shifting our thinking can be hard. Once our mind is firmly rooted in a belief it can be hard to change our opinions on a topic. I'm not talking about changing one of your fundamental moral principles; those should be firmly rooted in who you are and what you believe (like your faith in God, being against animal cruelty, believing all children deserve an education). What I am talking about is something that for years—possibly decades—was believed to be true, but now new research and data show that there is a better and different way.

As our society evolves, we discover and uncover new information that can turn conventional wisdom on its head. For example, ask my mom how she put my brother and me down to sleep as babies and she'll tell you "on your stomach." Fast forward thirty years later and new information shows we need to put babies down on their backs to sleep. I practiced this new advice with my kids despite the way it worked for my mom all those years ago.

Unfortunately, it's human nature to resist new information about any subject. But couple that with a topic that has been taught one way for decades (and decades)—like "asking is the only way to generate referrals"—and many people will dig their heels in and stick with the old way of thinking.

I encourage you not to be one of them.

Be open, because not only will I teach you why it's wrong to ask for referrals (including unpacking the experts' advice), I will show you the results others have had when they chose to go against conventional wisdom and were open to a new and different way. This new and different way is also easier, allows you to be authentic and provides results. (And let's be honest, does any of this matter if it doesn't work? No, so read on because what I will show you does work.)

Let's dive in and unleash your referral explosion.

Chapter
One

THE JOURNEY STARTS WITH FAILURE

Sometimes the best lessons are learned through trial and error. But not everyone needs to experience that same trial and error for a lesson to be understood and then applied in their own business (or life). We just need to be open to learn those lessons from a person who's experienced it.

I am by no means the first to learn some hard lessons through a business failure. I am actually in excellent company. According to Bloomberg, eight out of ten businesses fail within their first eighteen months. The lessons I learned when my first business failed have made all the difference in growing successful business #2.

My first business was an HR (human resources) consulting firm with big-name clients. Clients like KPMG, Snyder's Lance, BDO USA, Ally Bank, Coca-Cola Bottling Consolidated and others. When I list some of the clients I had, it's hard for people to believe the business failed.

My current business is a coaching, training and consulting practice teaching small business owners, solopreneurs and business development professionals how to grow their business through referrals without asking, how to establish loyalty-building, "sticky" client experiences and how to work smarter.

The ways in which my business #2 is different and stronger than business #1 all comes down to applying the lessons I learned when business #1 failed. Let's go back to the beginning for a quick overview and to uncover the most important lesson I learned from my business failure.

MY STORY

In 2007 I decided to take the entrepreneurial leap and leave my safe W-2 job to join a small company where I would come in as a partner and run and manage a new division in line with my HR expertise. A year later I had a client encourage me to leave the small firm and start my own company, to hang out my own "shingle," my first business shingle. That encouraging client would become my first and largest client for two years. Until they weren't, and then I had to quickly start bringing in new clients to survive. It didn't end well, and I wish I could blame the recession. But that wouldn't be true.

I remember the moment I looked at my husband, Norm, and uttered the words, "We need for me to get a job." Norm is very supportive so instead of saying what he *had* to be thinking and was the truth, he instead said, "We'll figure it out." But I knew I needed to make this painful decision and make it for us.

A few days later as I was starting my car to head to a networking event, a friend called about a position at a financial services company with a fancy title, Chief Talent Officer. As I pulled out of the driveway, I heard myself start asking questions about the job—like what is the CEO like (who would be my boss)? and what is the company culture?—and it hit me. That shingle I was so proud to hang when I started my business had now smacked me right in the stomach, like a sucker punch, and it took my breath away. I knew then that I was really going back to a nine-to-five, W-2 job. My entrepreneurial dream had died.

After months and months of reflection after the business failure, and through talking to other successful business owners, I discovered where it all went wrong. One primary shortcoming was that I hadn't established a system to bring in new clients *in a way that worked for me.*

With my HR consulting firm, probably not much different than your business or firm, clients had to know, like and trust me before they would hire me. In addition, they were more willing to take the recommendation of a colleague than just randomly finding me on the internet. Which meant that all that "brand and credibility" building I did for my first two years in business was for naught. (Not even my articles published in impressive magazines like *Accounting Today* or *Workforce Management* magazine or my interview with Bloomberg News could save me.)

What I needed—but didn't have—was a way to build a pipeline of prospective new clients so I could turn those prospects into clients. I was, of course, familiar with the old school business development techniques, but those didn't work well for me. They did work, but not well and not consistently. I ultimately worked too hard for each client I did land using those techniques. Those methods included incessant networking, free speaking engagements, direct mail and cold emails.

While all businesses need to employ some (or maybe all) of those techniques, plus others, when starting out, I was still using them four years later and not hitting the traction and volume I needed for my business to survive. Having a business development technique that works well for you is key for two reasons. First, you'll actually bring in revenue-producing clients. Second, if you go with techniques or tactics that you are willing to do, you'll do just that—use them to consistently produce results.

CRACKING THE REFERRAL CODE

On my quest to identify a few techniques, or sales activities, for building a pipeline of prospects, I decided to look a little deeper at referrals. All my early clients with my failed HR consulting firm had come as a result of hard-core networking or speaking gigs, not referrals. Discovering this was a light bulb moment for me and I wanted to know why. I had always known about referrals but not necessarily how to leverage them or have referrals be a consistent way to generate new clients. And when I say consistent, I mean, I could count on the tactic to generate new clients month in and month out, year in and year out.

My research into referrals—how they worked and how to leverage them—left me wanting…greatly. I didn't like what I found. It didn't fit me, my values, and it left me feeling inauthentic. The basic premise of the advice out there on generating referrals is to ask. You know what I'm talking about…the good ole-fashioned way of just asking someone to send you a client. Asking in every situation. Asking all the time. Asking the right people. Asking the wrong people. JUST ASK.

But that asking advice and the scripts to use when asking go against and contradict what a referral actually is—a connection made by a trusted friend, peer or colleague to connect one person who has a problem or a need to the person who can solve that problem or meet that need. You *can't* ask your way into those types of connections.

I was disappointed. Because asking for a referral feels an awful lot like making a cold call. They could almost be cousins. Think about it. Here is how the scenario goes for a cold call. I call you asking you to buy my product or service, or at least take a meeting to discuss buying my product/service. But I don't know if you're interested. Or if you care. And I interrupted your day for my needs only. *(And before some cold-calling professional chimes in to disagree—you can convince yourself all you want that ultimately you will make their business or life better by interrupting them. Please. If their problem was that bad they would have started seeking a solution on their own, more than likely through a recommendation, not a cold call. But I digress.)*

> **BECAUSE ASKING FOR A REFERRAL FEELS AN AWFUL LOT LIKE MAKING A COLD CALL. THEY COULD ALMOST BE COUSINS.**

Asking for a referral is the same as a cold call but instead of asking you to buy my product, I ask you to give me the name of someone you know who may need what I offer—my product or service. How do I know if the person you send me is interested? If they even care? And do they want their day interrupted to meet with me? And what will the person think of you when I tell them you gave me their name?

Asking for referrals, like cold calling, didn't work for me. But I loved the basic premise behind what a referral represented, what it stood for (which I'll get into more later) and what referrals could mean for my business. I wasn't ready to give up just yet and go looking for another business development solution.

So I set out to crack the code on generating referrals *without* asking, and crack it I did. Between business #1 (HR consulting firm) and business #2, I had some time to think, mainly while I worked at the corporate job I had to take after my business failure. By the time I left that job and started business #2, I had a basic concept of how my referral strategy would work. That referral strategy was created by sheer necessity; another business failure could not be in my future (particularly a failure caused because I ignored lessons already learned).

I didn't know if my referral plan would work. It was just a shell of an idea and I knew the only way to test it was to put it into action. I knew it would need refining, but based on my research and studying how companies developed business I knew it had a shot to work. **But it did better than just work…I had crazy success.**

I have been able to generate triple digit referrals (more than a hundred) every year, starting in 2014 through today. In my first year alone as a business coach I generated 112 referrals that I did not ask for. When demand for my coaching services went up, supply (my availability) went down and my clients noticed. It was harder to get on my schedule and they wanted to know why. So I started teaching my clients my referral process and they started having the same success. In some cases, better success than mine.

It seems they were hungry for a solution to generate business in the easiest way possible, but in a way that they could also feel authentic doing it. What a novel concept! Generating referrals is that solution, but only if you know how to do it without asking. I love helping people realize it is easier than you think once you know what to do. You could say I'm obsessed with all things referrals and you'd be right. But the reason I'm obsessed is because after years of testing my method on myself and my clients, I figured out how to take the guesswork out of generating referrals without asking.

When you remove the guesswork and start to have referral success, you—as the business owner—can focus on what you do best. And I'm guessing what you do best is the work you do for your clients, delivering value, being a partner and a resource (your sweet spot). This allows you to separate yourself from others in your industry, and you never have to worry about being seen as the "always hustling salesperson." When you're in a business where prospects have to know, like and trust you to decide to work with you, then your business should be sustained by referrals you never had to ask for. Because when referrals are your consistent business development tactic, you get to spend more time in your sweet spot—being the expert your clients have come to trust.

WHO IS SERVED BEST BY REFERRALS?

Every business in every industry can benefit from referrals, but it can seem easier for some businesses than others. It can seem that some businesses generate a ton of referrals without even trying, while others are left to wonder why they never receive referrals. If you are in the latter group (or want to increase the number of referrals you do receive), don't worry, there is a solution and this book will serve you well.

The businesses that seem to effortlessly generate referrals are more than likely the type that operate in a marketplace that's not crowded—like being the only one or "game" in town, a niche business—or they have built a solid reputation over decades and decades. Take Kate for example. She's an attorney, which in most cities is a very crowded marketplace, but her focus of law—elder law—isn't that crowded. It is easier for her to make a name for herself. Since she is one of a few that does what she does, other attorneys and financial advisors naturally reach out to her for her expertise because their clients need her. If Kate was just a wills, trusts and estates attorney or a divorce attorney she would be competing with hundreds of attorneys in her area (more likely thousands depending on the size of her city). But her specialty allows her to capture referrals because she is one of only a few.

The second type of business, one that operates in a crowded marketplace, is more than likely your type of business. It certainly was my type of business as a business coach. I was one of hundreds of coaches in town, not in a niche, and I was just getting started in the business. I had no track record. I didn't have decades of being known as "the best business coach." But I still generated 112 referrals in my first year in business.

Being in a crowded marketplace and wanting to grow your business are probably two of the reasons you picked up this book. My type of business—maybe like yours—is what I refer to as a "dime a dozen" profession; many people who do what you do. Some examples are financial advisors, realtors (residential and commercial), business and life coaches, CPAs, attorneys, property and casualty insurance agents, commercial bankers, interior designers, home builders, bookkeepers, photographers, business brokers and there are many more.

If you operate in a saturated marketplace is it harder to generate referrals? Yes. Impossible? Oh, absolutely NOT. If you are in a saturated marketplace and want an effective way to make generating referrals easier, then you have come to the right place. Particularly if you want to generate those referrals without ever asking for them.

The professions I listed above—and numerous others—are frequently operating in crowded marketplaces but they have something else in common. They must create relationships with their prospective clients. Your prospects not only have to know you and like you, they must also trust you. As Stephen M. R. Covey states in his book *Speed of Trust*, "The trust we have in people…comes, in part, from believing that they do care." It's pretty hard to build a relationship with someone if you don't believe they care about you on some level. Most of us started our relationship-based business because we are good at helping people in a specific area and we care about our clients.

In business, trust is the real currency and relationships are the economic driver. Without trust no one buys from you, stays with you or becomes a repeat client. And at the heart of a referral is trust. When you understand what a referral is, coupled with its power, you hold the key to generating a consistent stream of referrals in your business. So, let's make sure we are clear on the why and the what.

> IN BUSINESS, TRUST IS THE REAL CURRENCY AND RELATIONSHIPS ARE THE ECONOMIC DRIVER.

At the end of some of the chapters you will find resources listed under the Chapter Download section. You can download those resources at www. generatingbusinessreferrals.com/resources.

Chapter Two

WHAT A REFERRAL *REALLY* IS AND WHAT IT ISN'T

When I say the word "referral," what comes to mind? There's a right and a wrong answer to this question. What I find is that most people confuse the definition of referral with other types of prospect or lead generation terms, like "warm lead." The confusion with these terms (or sales lingo) has allowed the definition of a referral to become extremely diluted today. Most sales lingo generalizes different types of lead generation and unfortunately groups together terms because they *seem* similar. Terms like "introduction" and "word of mouth buzz" are explained to be the same as a referral. But nothing could be further from the truth. Let's first look at why referrals are so powerful and then define the different sales lingo through examples.

THE POWER OF REFERRALS

Referrals are the most powerful source of generating clients for a few key reasons. You don't have to go looking for that client; they drop in your lap (or your email inbox); they are less price sensitive and value your product or service before you tell them about it; and they are quicker to close because they have "bought you" before meeting you.

How is this possible? Because of the transfer of trust—the real currency in business—between the person referring you (who I call the referral source) and the prospective new client, the person who needs your product or service. When the prospective new client identifies a need, or the referral source points out their need to them, they enter a mindset of wanting to meet that need. At that moment the prospective new client starts thinking about who could solve the problem and wants a recommendation from someone they trust. This mentality is the basis of why, according to Nielsen research, 83 percent of people prefer to make buying decisions based on a recommendation from a friend, family member or someone they trust.

> **83 PERCENT OF PEOPLE PREFER TO MAKE BUYING DECISIONS BASED ON A RECOMMENDATION FROM A FRIEND, FAMILY MEMBER OR SOMEONE THEY TRUST.**

TRUST

Trust cannot be artificially created, and you cannot buy it. It must be developed and nurtured. So when the referral source tells their friend, family member or colleague that you are the right person to solve their problem, their pain, they trust that advice. Why? Because they trust the person recommending the solution. Which means when that prospect meets with you—as the provider to solve their need—you reap the benefits of that "referral source-prospect" trust, and it's transferred to you automatically. But a word of caution: Even though the referred prospect is "ready to go" and has trust in you, you still must develop the know-like-trust factor more before they may be ready to say yes to working with you. You still need to determine if you can help them and if they are the right fit for your service/product.

The reason referrals are easier to close, quicker to close and less price sensitive is because of the transferred trust from a referral source to the prospect about you and your ability to solve their problem. They have a need, they trust you to solve it, and your obligation at that moment is to make sure you *can* solve it (or find another resource for them). Plus, you're sure you can do great work. You also need to thank and nurture the referral source who delivered you a "ready to go" client, but we'll get to that a little bit later. Next, we need to make sure we understand exactly what a referral is and what it is not.

DEFINING SALES LINGO

Being introduced to someone is not necessarily the same as being referred to someone. And even though someone spoke *really* highly of you to a friend yesterday (word of mouth buzz) it doesn't mean it's a referral. I see people confuse and misuse three main terms—warm lead, introduction and word of mouth buzz—as the same as a referral.

So how do you know the difference? How do you know what is a real referral? Let me break it down for you. Let's start by defining warm lead, introduction, word of mouth buzz and referral.

WARM LEAD

Please note, there is a difference between a cold lead and a warm lead. A cold lead is a prospect you found "cold," meaning they never showed an interest in hearing from you or being contacted by you; you just reached out "cold" without any prompts from them. This is where the term "cold calling" or "cold emailing" comes from. Most people do not confuse a cold lead with a referral, but they will confuse a warm lead as a referral, so it's important to know the difference.

Definition: When someone you know tells you a company may need your service or product and possibly even gives you permission to use their name when you follow up with that company. They may or may not provide a contact name; but either way it is still a warm lead.

Example: "Hi, Stacey. I know that XYZ company could really use your help and your services/product. The contact is Tom and here's his number. When you call him, use my name."

INTRODUCTION

Definition: The person connecting you with a possible new client introduces you to each other (normally via email) but doesn't state you should explore working together. They typically use words like "synergy," "great connection," or "you are two people who should know each other."

Example: "Ed, meet Stacey Randall, and Stacey, meet Ed Smith. You two are great people and should know each other. Happy connecting."

WORD OF MOUTH BUZZ

Definition: When people tell you they have mentioned you or talked about you to others. They may even share what they said, like how awesome you are, how you helped them, or they highlight the results they experienced by working with you.

Example: "Hey, Stacey. I was talking to my client Dan the other week about how you have helped me. He'll reach out."

REFERRAL

Definition: When you're connected with a potential new client by someone (the referral source) and they say that the potential new client expressed a need (problem, pain point) they know you can help them with.

Example: "Stacey, I have copied Cindi on this email. She and I were talking the other day about her need to grow referrals in her business and I instantly thought of you. I told her I would connect you two so you can talk about how you might help her."

Okay, looking at the definitions and examples of the three sales terms (warm lead, introduction and word of mouth buzz), can you see the difference between them and the definition of a referral? At the heart of a referral are two key points the other terms don't have: (1.) the personal connection made between you and the prospect by the referral source and (2.) the prospect's need was identified by the referral source. (See Figure A.)

SALES TERM	NEED IDENTIFIED	CONNECTION MADE
Warm Lead	No	No
Introduction	No	Yes
Word of Mouth Buzz	Yes	No
Referral	Yes	Yes

Figure A

In short, how you are positioned by the referral source is what makes a referral an actual referral. The referral source needs to connect you with the prospect, and they need to share why they are connecting you—because the prospective client has a need that you can solve. A connection made and a need identified… without these two points you don't have a referral. Let's dive a

A CONNECTION MADE AND A NEED IDENTIFIED...WITHOUT THESE TWO POINTS YOU DON'T HAVE A REFERRAL.

little deeper and uncover just what keeps a warm lead, word of mouth buzz or an introduction from being a referral.

UNDERSTANDING THE SEPARATION FACTOR

WHAT KEEPS A WARM LEAD FROM BEING A REFERRAL?

Example: "Hi, Stacey. I know that XYZ company could really use your help and your services/product. The contact is Tom and here's his number. When you call him, use my name."

A warm lead is lacking both connection and a need identified. Let's look at the connection that is lacking: There is no connection to the person who may need your services or products. While being able to use someone's name is better than not being able to (which is what makes this a warm lead versus a cold lead), the person who provided the lead didn't make a connection to, in this example, Tom at XYZ Company.

In my experience I have found there are a few common reasons for not making the connection. For example, what they heard about Tom and his need is actually just a rumor, so they aren't 100 percent sure there is a real need. Or they think the company needs you, but the company doesn't know that or think that yet. Or they did talk to Tom about his need, but it was a while ago and at this point they don't want to go back to Tom with your name as a possible solution. Or they won't put their name on the line (in writing via an email) for you to Tom, this one is the biggest concern of all.

I have had people provide me with warm leads in the past. They mean well, but closing a warm lead can be just as hard as closing a cold lead. Usually the person thinks highly of what I do and knows I could help the company, but they aren't in a position to help the company figure it out or point out that the company has a problem—identify the need—and they aren't comfortable making the connection. For them, the next best thing they can do is to let me know about it. But again, their information is a warm lead, not a referral, and shouldn't be treated like one.

WHAT PREVENTS AN INTRODUCTION FROM BEING A REFERRAL?

<u>Example:</u> "Ed, meet Stacey Randall, and Stacey, meet Ed Smith. You two are great people and should know each other. Happy connecting."

Typically, an introduction comes through email but it can also be made face to face at an event of some kind (like a business networking or charity event). If the introduction is made at an event, to keep the connection you will need to get the business card or contact information for the prospective client (in our example above, Ed Smith) for the connection to continue. But while the referral source has made a connection between Ed and me, there is not an expressed need to work together. By not saying it, that we should explore working together, the intended referral just became an introduction. Which makes it harder to set the first meeting and once meeting you then have extra work to do to establish why you are meeting in the first place. Positioning is key, and positioning is set by the referral source when they establish or identify the need (the reason for Ed to meet with me).

Now, it is true that plenty of introductions aren't intended to be referrals. They are meant to be just that…an introduction, an opportunity for you to meet someone to grow your network. Less likely is also an introduction that might help the referral source by you agreeing to meet with the person they introduce to you to. It is important for you to know the difference so you can respond accordingly. If the introduction is meant to be just an introduction, then you do have the ability and right to protect your time and, possibly, decide not to meet with Ed. But knowing the intent does allow you to make a better-informed decision on why you are meeting.

WHAT KEEPS WORD OF MOUTH BUZZ FROM BEING A REFERRAL?

<u>Example:</u> "Hey, Stacey. I was talking to my client Dan the other week about how you have helped me. He'll reach out."

Word of mouth buzz always identifies the need of the prospect; it has come up in a conversation between the referral source and the prospect. It is why your name then comes up as part of the conversation. It's because of the work you do and how you might help. But in the example above, the referral source did not connect me with Dan via email (which is the preferred way to connect) so that I can reach out to him. While the referral source did the heavy lifting—identifying the need of the prospect—I still have to do my part. My part is to follow up and schedule a meeting with Dan, if he is willing. But because the referral source didn't connect me with Dan he removed me from the driver's seat of moving the sales process along. And if I can't follow up, my chances of connecting will be extremely limited.

Without an email connection, it's unlikely that Dan will reach out. The referral source believes that since Dan has my contact information, he will contact me. But we know there's a greater chance he will lose my information or just forget. And the longer his follow-up is delayed the chance are less likely he'll remember to follow up. Why? Because the conversation is no longer top of mind. And surprisingly it won't be because Dan doesn't want to explore working together, but Dan is busy and his "busyness" usually wins out. Most likely, Dan will forget. Just human nature. So to help Dan out, we need the referral source to make the connection in addition to identifying the need.

After describing what word of mouth buzz really is, I once heard someone describe it as the "lazy man's referral," meaning they want the credit for "referring" to you but didn't want to do any of the work to make it happen. It's funny but not always true; usually the referral source isn't being intentionally lazy. The conversation happened spontaneously but the referral source still needs a little directing from you on how to make the referral happen—in this case, connecting me with Dan.

Of course, some word of mouth buzz may flip itself into a referral. Meaning that Dan will actually follow up and let you know who told him about you. Those situations are more rare, but they do happen and are awesome, of course.

***

To quickly re-cap, a warm lead lacks making the connection and identifying the need. An introduction lacks identifying the need but does make a connection. And a warm lead identifies the need but doesn't making the connection. I would argue that making the connection is the easy part; the harder part, the more important part, is identifying the need with the prospect.

KEEP THE FOCUS ON REFERRALS

While I am not a fan of warm leads, I'm certainly not against introductions and word of mouth buzz. But to be clear, they aren't referrals. Remember, to be a referral, the key is for the **trust** the referral source has in you as the solution must be transferred to the prospect. That can only be done by stating why we should meet and by making the connection.

Now I've gotten pretty good with how I respond to warm leads, introductions and word of mouth buzz and my responses are now just part of my process. But in the beginning I lost a lot of opportunities and wasted a lot of time on "let's grab coffee and see where this goes" networking meetings. At first I didn't have a strategic response for the referral source to turn an introduction or word of mouth buzz into a solid referral. Once I developed my response, my ability to flip an introduction or word of mouth buzz into a referral increased significantly.

But what about those warm leads? I would also always thank someone for a warm lead but never follow up, and I would let the referral source know why I wouldn't be following up. I would use a strategic response to try to flip the warm lead into a referral; however the success rate for that method is much lower for all the reasons warm leads aren't generally helpful. (See

"What keeps a warm lead from being a referral" on the previous pages). Remember, following up on a warm lead is almost as unproductive as cold calling. As my business grew with more and more clients coming through referrals (now 90-95 percent), I abandoned the attempt to flip warm leads into referrals. This saved me extra time and effort. But in the beginning, as you work to grow your business through referrals, learning to flip a warm lead into a referral could be a good use of your time. Only you know for sure.

So now you know the difference between referrals, word of mouth buzz, introductions and warm leads. If you want to grow your business, use this new understanding to build responses to turn all introductions, word of mouth buzz and warm leads into referrals.

The final piece of the foundation of referrals is understanding where referrals actually come from. You now understand a referral's power and what constitutes a *real* referral. Before we move on let's make sure we know where referrals come from so we can leverage those sources.

WHERE REFERRALS COME FROM

Referrals come from two main sources and a more sporadic third source. The two principle sources are your clients and your centers of influence (COI). Your COI is a distinct group of people who are not clients but they know what you do, come in contact with your ideal client and don't do what you do so there is not competitive overlap. Your COI is a targeted group within your overall professional (and sometimes personal) network.

The third more sporadic source is your general professional network. In my experience, I have found that some people in your general network who refer to you unexpectedly can be cultivated to become a COI who refers to you, if you know what to do. But most likely when the stars align and one person from your greater network randomly sends you a prospective client; unfortunately, the odds of them doing it again are not likely. In other words, your general network is sporadic when it comes to generating referrals for you.

This means that your focus needs to be on cultivating referrals from the two main sources—your clients and COI. But not all businesses will receive referrals from both sources. Take my client Amanda, for example. She is a personal injury attorney. As you can imagine, she doesn't focus on generating referrals from her clients. When you become Amanda's client, typically the worst thing imaginable just happened to you or a loved one—injury or death. Amanda is not interested in constantly reminding her clients of the time they worked with her because they do associate that time in their life with pain and loss. Now, of course, if a client ever knows someone who may need Amanda they don't hesitate to refer the person to her. She does incredible work and her clients appreciate her service to them. But her focus on generating referrals is through her COI, which consists of other attorneys. She is willing to allow client referrals to just happen.

It's a different story for Terry and Michelle, who own a property and casualty insurance firm. Their referral strategy is to generate both client referrals and COI referrals for their two lines of business—personal and commercial. They also focus on generating a large volume of referrals; therefore having a plan to generate referrals from both sources—clients and COI—is the key to reaching the volume they need.

My business receives most referrals from existing clients with some strong COI mixed in. Funny, many of my COI eventually become clients. So how dependent you will be on one source or another (or both) depends on your business and referral needs. From working with my clients, I have found that the easiest referrals to close do come from clients because they intimately know what it is like to work with you, so their trust factor with the prospect is typically higher than with a COI. But a COI who can speak to the work you do and has referred others to you who are happy, is the next best referral source. It can also help if your COI referral source is in a position of being a trusted resource or advisor to the prospect they are referring because they are more likely to follow their advice.

Sometimes you may receive referrals from someone you don't know. For example, I once received a referral for my coaching service from a therapist I had never met and did not know (I had never even heard her name before). But if you do some digging you will discover that typically a client, a COI or someone in your general network recommended you. In this case the therapist had reached out to her network asking for a resource for a client and someone in her network gave her my name. It's important to try to learn the source who referred you whenever possible; knowing who referred you is step one in the process of generating more referrals (but more on that later). You also need to know the other people in the referral process and the role they play.

DEFINING THE PLAYERS

To truly leverage the power of referrals in your business it is helpful for you to know who the characters or players are in the referral process. There are three key players in the referral process, and they each play a unique part in the process. And like any good story with characters, there can be only one hero.

The three players:

- The referral source
- The prospect (prospective new client)
- You, the service provider or product

The unique role each player brings are:

- The referral source—carries the trust that your service can solve the problem.
- The prospect—has the actual need or problem that needs to be solved.
- You, the service provider—have the solution to the need or problem.

So can you guess who the hero is?

If you guessed the prospect or yourself, as the service provider, you would be wrong. Sorry. The hero of the referral process is the referral source. They matter the most in this process. Yes, it's great that the prospect will have their problem solved (and life or business made better) by hiring you, but that doesn't make them the most important person in this process. That you will gain another new client and have the chance to help them by solving their problem is just bonus a for you. You may be the most grateful in this process, but that doesn't make you the hero.

The referral source is the hero of this process because their

THE HERO OF THE REFERRAL PROCESS IS THE REFERRAL SOURCE.

actions allow the most critical part of the referral equation to happen. That part of the equation is when the referral source's trust in you is transferred to the prospect. Remember, trust is the real currency of business, which is fueled by relationships and cannot be bought. It must be earned, and when the referral source tells the prospect that you can solve their problem, the referral source wants to be right. The referral source only refers prospects to people they trust and have a relationship with on some level.

Now that we are clear on what a referral is and who the players are in the process, let's look at the decades-old advice on how to generate referrals by asking. Understanding the "old" way may help us see why a new approach is needed.

<u>Chapter Download</u>: Sales Lingo Defined Cheat Sheet
To download please visit:
www.generatingbusinessreferrals.com/resources

Chapter
Three

BUT WE'VE ALWAYS TAUGHT IT THAT WAY!

I f you search the internet for information on how to receive more referrals or how to grow your business by increasing referrals you will find plenty of advice. Trouble is it's not necessarily good advice. Most of the advice sounds extremely similar—same tactics, same tips, same game plan to follow.

What's more troubling is that this advice has been around for a long time, and it keeps getting re-used, re-purposed and re-sold. Just because the advice is old and has been around for a long time doesn't mean it's the right advice for you. Back in the Introduction I told you that to increase your referral success you would need to be prepared to shift your thinking from the conventional advice that exists on how to generate more referrals. In fact, a lot of the advice is counterproductive to actually growing a business—long term and with sustainability—

through referrals. The age-old advice is not working and we know it, so we aren't using it. Why?

- Because it doesn't feel right.
- It strikes us as off-putting.
- It comes across as very one-sided.
- It seems "salesy" and inauthentic.
- It makes us feel like we are begging.

How do we know the approach isn't ideal? Because when we consider having someone use those same tactics on us we cringe, shudder and trust that pit in our stomach screaming "find the door and get away." Okay, so maybe not that dramatic but we shift uncomfortably in our chairs and try to wrap up the conversation. We know we are about to give a response the person won't want to hear, which is "I'll think about it." We say, "I'll think about it," because we know it'll wrap up the conversation. In reality, we can't just snap our fingers and have people on the ready to refer. We know when someone asks us for a referral, it is not that often that we instantly know people who have a problem and are ready to have it solved.

In addition, because we don't respond favorably to the person who uses this method on us, most of us are uncomfortable using those same tactics on someone else. It's the Golden Rule: Do unto others as you would have them do unto you. Or in this case, don't do to others what you don't want done to you. Because we don't like asking or when others ask us, we then leap to the conclusion that a business grown and supported by referrals is just not possible for us.

Time and time again the top piece of advice given about how to increase or get more referrals is to "ASK." Which is then supported by all the many ways you can ask:

- the exact right times to ask
- the different scripts to use
- the printed and digital materials to support your ask (or perpetuate your ask)
- and worst of all…how if you can't ask or are unwilling to ask, then you have head trash issues that you need to overcome.

Book after book, article after article and blog post after blog post share the same few tactics to increase your referrals by asking. And we aren't buying it. For good reason. Because we know the truth. People don't refer us to make our jobs easier, make us more money or help our business grow. And they don't refer just because we asked.

People refer to help someone they care about who is in need, and they know their friend's need can be solved by our service or product. Someone giving us a referral is not about us, and *asking for a referral makes it all about us.* Herein lies the conflict and is why asking doesn't work.

> SOMEONE GIVING US A REFERRAL IS NOT ABOUT US, AND **ASKING FOR A REFERRAL MAKES IT ALL ABOUT US.**

Asking for referrals goes against the fundamental truth of why referrals happen.

So why do the experts keep telling us to ask? Great question. It all boils down to one key reason. Asking for a referral, in their opinion, gets you closest to the money, the next sale, the next closed deal, the next new client. Many experts believe that asking for referrals is the fastest way to generate new clients, which leads to sales. And since that is what everyone wants—"get me to the promised land of more clients as fast as possible"—the experts provide the simplest route to get there.

Asking feels and looks like instant activity, and any salesperson knows that activity is typically what is tracked and measured since in the sales process we don't control the outcome. But instant activity is worthless if it doesn't yield results, particularly the results you want. It can be hard to be patient, but to generate referrals you need to focus on building relationships, which takes time. I have had many students go through my Growth By Referrals program and generate referrals quickly but that isn't guaranteed. Like Gray, managing partner of the CPA firm, who generated twenty referrals in just a few months. Or Michelle, who owns a property and casualty insurance company, who generated eighty-three referrals in just one quarter.

Asking may feel like you are taking action, but that action probably won't produce the results you want over the long term. Generating referrals is its own separate plan, a referral generating plan, and it should be separate from a prospecting or sales plan and separate from a marketing plan. If you are looking for instant activity then focus on the tactics within your prospecting plan—like networking, direct mail, reaching out to prospects, buying leads, among others.

But the truth is, asking won't serve you well in the long term. And I would argue that it doesn't serve you well in the short term either. Because if it did work we would all be doing it…*every day.* But when we think about asking we hesitate, get uncomfortable, and can acknowledge that asking for a referral puts a lot of pressure on the person we are asking. Why? Well, we need to understand what drives our referral sources to understand why asking doesn't work.

WHAT DRIVES THE HERO

Remember, the referral source is our hero. It is important to understand what really drives the hero to make the connection to you for the prospect. Why the hero refers people to people he or she trusts is actually all about him (or her), but for a really good reason that comes from a really good place.

In our brains we have an area called the hypothalamus, which regulates some of our needs (like thirst and hunger) and some of our behaviors. When we help others, the hypothalamus is affected and creates feelings of pleasure that we want to repeat. In a sense, the hypothalamus drives our need to belong, feel connected and matter to others. One way to feel as if we matter to others is to help them.

So when a referral source—the hero—connects someone they know or care about to you, when they refer you a new client, they do it because the person they know needs help and helping that person allows them to feel good about themselves. Now they can only feel good about helping a friend or colleague in need if they believe you are the right person to provide the help through your service or product. This is why a referral can't be manufactured or artificially created by asking or paying for it; what drives the hero must be real. The triggering of their human need to help is critical for them to repeat the process because at the heart of a referral is one person helping another person who is in need.

Knowing that a referred potential client arrives with an established level of trust in us, transferred from the referral source, makes this trust sacred and it cannot be violated. It is the "why" behind the referral; you can help someone they know so they refer you. It is also why people prefer to have a recommendation for a service provider or product before they purchase. They want to have someone they trust help them with the decision. As Parthiv Shah, author of *Business Kamasutra, From Persuasion to Pleasure*, explains so perfectly, "Most aim for sales. Few aim to create relationships that drive sales."

Remember the referral philosophy: referrals come from relationships. Which is why advice from experts to ask and find clever ways to facilitate the ongoing ask just doesn't work. Over the years we have received bad "asking for referrals" advice like the following. As you read through each of them you will now be able to see how the tactics won't generate true referrals.

- Memorize a referral script to ask at the end of meetings and during all interactions with every customer, COI and prospect.

- Create referral cards about you for your clients and referral sources to hand out to people who may need your services.
- Create a list of people your clients may know (list of colleagues, people in Rotary) and ask them to make specific introductions so they can be sent a book or audio interview you created, sometimes called a referral package.
- Add to your newsletter that you are "Open for business and accepting referrals."
- Craft a letter for your referral source to send out to all their clients sharing something of value you provide and offering to make an introduction.
- Ask for referrals from prospects…the prospect might not be ready to buy but know someone who is.
- Establish a referral promotion: For every referral we'll give you $25 or a new TV or whatever.
- Add to your email signature "The greatest compliment you can provide is a referral."
- Join a leads group where "referring" each other is mandatory. (If it is mandatory to refer you, it violates the very foundation of why I would refer you.)
- Include in the contract or agreement new clients sign a requirement for the number of referrals that *must* be provided to you, in addition to what they are going to pay you for your service.
- Give them a stack of books or digital file copies of an audio interview that they can pass on to those they know who might need your services.

- Capitalize on reciprocity, which is the desire we feel to help others after they helped us. (Except that this is twisted to take advantage of the happiness or relief a new client feels when they agree to work with you. Just for the record, the client doesn't owe you or me anything except payment for a job done.)
- Overcome your own "head trash" and just ask. (This one, in my opinion, is particularly dangerous.)

I urge you to not fall for these tactics. While one or two of these may work sporadically for you they won't generate ongoing referrals. When I work with my clients through my Growth By Referrals program to put in place their referral generating plan, I am actually more concerned with how many referrals they receive three years from now as opposed to just three months from now. The truth is you don't have to ask or employ the tactics above to cultivate referrals. [Insert sigh of relief here.]

Now there is some advice in these books that is good. But there are fundamental suggestions that just don't work. What I offer is a different perspective based on my research, direct experience and my clients' experiences; it is rooted in success, where taking advantage of a client's reciprocity isn't necessary, asking with the help of scripts isn't necessary, creating a referral gimmick isn't necessary. As you will learn as you complete this book, I provide a more comprehensive approach to generating referrals that allows you to avoid feeling inauthentic and manipulative.

What most referral books have in common, and where we agree, is on the power of referrals, how they are the gold standard to growing your business, how they are easier to close to become new clients, and the need for the know, like and trust factor. What is different between most books and the one you are holding is how you apply the knowledge of what a referral is and how you take action to generate referrals.

For example, you should not have an expectation that you are owed referrals from anyone. Yes, you may deserve referrals but you are not owed them, and your attitude and behavior towards those who could send you referrals shouldn't be one of expectation. It's never a good idea to take advantage of the feeling someone has toward you when they decide to work with you—called reciprocity—by using, or in my opinion manipulating, the opportunity to ask for referrals. And networking strategies, although you can use them to meet a lot of people, disguised as referral advice won't provide you with a system to develop relationships.

> **YOU MAY DESERVE REFERRALS BUT YOU ARE NOT OWED THEM**

Referrals come from relationships, relationships come from connections, and connections are maintained through ongoing touch points that keep you top of mind. Referrals don't come from asking, from manipulating situations or because you think you are owed them. So when you pick up a book on referrals use the information from those books that respect what a referral is and ignore the rest.

The ability to put the decades old "asking advice" in context and see it for what it is, is important. Let's look a little deeper at what happens to our referral source when we ask and when we pay for referrals.

WHY ASKING AND PAYING FOR REFERRALS IS WRONG

Have you ever asked for a referral? What happened?

Did the person you asked answer with a stock response like, "Let me think about it?" Or did they almost automatically sit back in their chair or start to shift in their seat? When they moved back from you they were subconsciously trying to distance themselves from the request you just made. And the shift in their chair means they are uncomfortable.

Why does that happen? Because you attempted to create a referral that doesn't exist. Let me explain. When you ask for a referral you attempt to manufacture the referral, or artificially create part of the referral that must occur naturally. The part of a referral that can't be made up, or manufactured, is the prospect having a real need, a real problem they need solved. When you ask someone for a referral they then have to figure out who has a need or problem you can solve. When you attempt to artificially create or manufacture the need, you force the referral process and once forced it never works.

Now, you could argue that asking allows the other person to start thinking about who to refer to you. Okay, let's go with that logic for a moment. Think back to a time when you asked someone for referrals, or the last time you were asked by someone to refer him or her to people you know.

Did the person you asked to send you referrals actually get back to you with a list of names of people *wanting to meet you*? And by "wanting to meet you," I mean that the list of people you were provided had their need identified, knew you and how your product or service could solve their problem, and they had agreed to be referred to you?

Same goes for you when you were asked to refer. Did you get back to the person with the names and contact information of your friends and colleagues? Did you identify they had a need and a desire to connect?

Almost 99 percent of the time the answer is no. People you ask to refer to you don't get back to you. They don't follow up with a list of ten—or heck even a few—people who want to meet with you to learn about your product or service, and they don't follow up to connect you to them. They just don't do it. And my guess is, when you were asked to refer you didn't get back to the person asking either.

In some cases you will hear back from the person you asked to send you referrals, but it won't be the response you were looking for. They give vague information (you know, first name with no last name) or tell you if the person is interested they will follow up with you directly. In some cases, they don't want you to use their name. (Sounds like your list of potential referrals just became a list of warm or even cold leads.) But more than likely they just won't get back to you and will hope you don't follow up. Let's look at this a little deeper. What happens when we do ask.

WHAT HAPPENS WHEN WE DO ASK?

A CLIENT MINI-CASE STUDY

Let me paint a picture from an experience one of my clients had. This client owns a CPA firm and we'll call him Jim. Last year he decided to reach out to each of his business owner clients after tax season was over to check in. Overall, he wanted to know how happy his clients were with his firm. So Jim developed a "client follow-up system document" that his team could use to guide them through the client calls. There were a few hundred calls to make, and the document made sure his team members asked each client the same questions.

His objective was to take a pulse on the "stickiness" of the client, get in front of any issues—if any—that needed to be resolved, uncover any upsell or cross-sell opportunities that he could follow up on later, ask for referrals and ask for testimonials.

The process was a resounding success…except for one part. Can you guess which part wasn't successful? Over 250 calls were made. Guess how many referrals they received from their direct ask?

One.

Only one referral, and according to Jim that referral deal—over a year later—still hadn't closed. Can you guess which question was removed from the "client follow-up document" for the next year? Yep, the referral question. Through the "client follow-up" process Jim received tons of awesome testimonials but only one referral. His clients were happy and agreed to put their name on their testimonial for his marketing needs, but they didn't provide any referrals. Why?

THE REALITY OF THE ASK

The direct ask is off-putting. When you ask me directly and I'm not ready for it you make me think, make me work; then I become uncomfortable when I can't come up with anyone. So I say something like, "Not at this time" or "Let me think about it and get back to you." But I don't.

The reason for my discomfort and then brushing off your request is because I now must figure out who may need your product or service. I have to sit down and think about people I could connect to you. I may come up with one or two people after you asked. But, long term, what you need and should want is a way to build a habit for referral sources to refer you without using "the ask" as a trigger.

Remember, the reason why referrals are so powerful is because the prospective new client has already identified their need (or at least the problem they would like to solve) and is open to meeting with someone who can solve their problem. You just can't manufacture this need by scrolling through your contacts on your phone looking for someone to refer. You have to know they have a need.

Remember, referrals are powerful because they are easier and usually faster to close, take less work to get them to the end of the buyer's journey and are less price-sensitive (meaning they add greater value to your service because you were referred to them). But all of these reasons (and others) as to why a referral is powerful rest on *the need* the prospective client has, the problem they want to solve. The need is real, and they'd prefer for someone they know to recommend the person/company they should work with.

Think about it. If you're a realtor does anyone really need to meet you unless they are in the market to buy or sell their home? What about a home builder? Unless someone wants to build a home, will they fill up their time with a meeting that doesn't really matter (no matter how awesome you are)? Same for a CPA, financial advisor, attorney, business consultant or almost any service-based business. Unless I am looking for what you offer I probably won't be willing to talk to you about doing business together even, if someone I trust says I should meet with you.

When you ask directly, you make the referral about you. And referrals aren't about you, they are about the person who may need your product or service. Which is why the gimmicks

> WHY A REFERRAL IS POWERFUL REST ON **THE NEED** THE PROSPECTIVE CLIENT HAS, THE PROBLEM THEY WANT TO SOLVE.

used by the experts don't work (more on that in Chapter 5) and why asking makes most people uncomfortable.

Back to Jim, our CPA firm owner. Here is the fascinating thing about Jim's business: he does receive referrals. Not as many as he wants or deserves, but on a small scale his clients do refer him. The referrals may only trickle in, but they do show up and have been for years, long before he created his client follow-up system.

So how is it that when you ask for a referral you hear crickets, but referrals still flow in? Some would argue that the direct ask Jim made planted a seed for future referrals. Not likely, since his trickle of referrals stayed as consistent after his ask as they were before his ask. Through all my work with clients, my personal experience and my research, asking directly actually has the opposite effect.

NEGATIVE CONSEQUENCES OF ASKING

When you ask, especially often, you gain a reputation in your clients' and your COIs' minds that you always have your hand out when they're around you. Even if you have only asked a few times, the perception quickly builds that each time they are with you, you are going to ask them, and they would rather not go through that time and again. It's the same situation with the salesperson who every time you see them—at a networking event, in a restaurant, even at the grocery store—they are going to try to sell you something, or at least get their business card in your hands. We all keep a mental list of who these people are and try to avoid them at all cost.

Have your ever considered what you would say to a person when you are making the third or fourth request for referrals? Even if a few months have gone by since you last asked, they probably remember the first time (and second and third time) you asked. Pretty soon you become that pesky person who is always asking. It makes you seem self-absorbed, annoying and in some cases inconsiderate of the other person's needs. I'm not saying you are those things (self-absorbed, annoying, etc.) when you ask over and over again, but it may well be how you come across.

Luckily for Jim, his ask for referrals didn't stop the few referral sources who had referred him in the past from continuing to refer him. But his overall referral numbers (on a yearly basis) had not increased. So, I asked him, "Who is referring you?" Jim responded with exactly what I expected.

- The clients he has a relationship with
- And one specific client who Jim helped save his business; that client became a raving, referring fan

Not many, but definitely a start for Jim to develop a consistent referral strategy. At the heart of the referral strategy needs to be creating relationship with clients and COIs who will then provide ongoing referrals. Jim's issue was that he was sporadic about maintaining his relationships with his referring clients and he wasn't actively trying to cultivate new referral sources. Missing out on these two opportunities had caused him to miss out on opportunities to capture referrals.

RECOGNIZING MISSED OPPORTUNITIES

Most of the advice out there on referrals is to "ask for what you need." But as we learned it doesn't work and can have negative consequences. But the experts keep pushing the "just ask" because of that one time when the ask did work.

Here is an example you've probably heard over and over to show how asking can work. You call a client and make a direct ask for referrals. The client responds with "come to think of it last week I met with Sally and she could use your help."

No! No! No! Want to know what this example really says about you?

That the client came across an opportunity where someone needed help—in the form of work you do—but he didn't think of you. You just happened to follow up while his conversation with Sally was still fresh in his mind, so he made the connection you could help Sally.

First, this rarely happens and second, I want it the other way around for you. I want you to be top of mind, in an authentic way, so when that client was meeting with Sally he said on the spot, "I know exactly who you need. It's _____ (insert your name) and I'll connect you two by email as soon as I get back to the office."

There is a difference. The latter is more powerful and, let's be honest, it requires less work on your part and your client's part. By making the connection in the moment it comes up that Sally needs you, your client doesn't have to go back to Sally after the moment has passed. When you're top of mind—through outreach you do for your referral sources—you reap amazing referral benefits.

I want more for you than…

- Asking more than 250 clients for a referral and only receiving one.
- Making a direct ask only to find out you're an afterthought.
- Asking for referrals only to hear crickets.
- Asking for referrals only to make those you know, and yourself, uncomfortable.

I want more for you and you should want more for yourself too. Here's the thing: You don't have to ask to receive referrals, but you can't get away with doing nothing either. In Chapter 11, I will explain how you set up receiving referrals by mastering what I call *referral seed planting*. It is crucial for you to understand *how* to plant seeds so future referrals can be cultivated. Now, referral seed planting is only one step in the process but one you will want to know.

PAYING FOR REFERRALS FEELS JUST LIKE ASKING

So what about paying for referrals? That is typically the question that follows the "Do I have to ask for referrals?" question. Let's unpack this one as well. There is a belief in the business world that to entice someone to send you business you should offer them compensation in the form of a kickback, sometimes called a referral fee. But entering into a paying arrangement changes the dynamic of the relationship with the referral source. Let's look at why.

A fascinating study was done in 1969 at Carnegie Mellon University by Ed Deci. Deci devised an experiment that asked college students to play a puzzle game called Soma.

The experiment asked two groups of students to play the game for a set amount of time. One group was not paid to solve the puzzles and one group was paid a dollar for each puzzle finished.

The experiment was focused on what happened after the students stopped playing with the puzzles when the allotted time was up. Through a one-way mirror Deci studied the actions of both groups. The first group, who was *not* paid to solve the puzzles, acted entirely different than the second group, who had been paid.

The first group, the group not paid, kept solving the puzzles after time was up. The second group stopped. According to Deci, "The money reward interfered with whatever intrinsic sense of challenge and enjoyment Soma might have provided for them."

Clearly the group who was offered no money to solve the puzzle had more fun. That's why they kept going. So let's apply this psychology to referrals. Referrals come from relationships, so when you pay for a referral you commoditize the relationship. Commoditization

WHEN YOU PAY FOR A REFERRAL YOU COMMODITIZE THE RELATIONSHIP.

is not a good thing. Let's put ourselves in the prospective new client's shoes (the person who had a need or pain and is being referred to you). Imagine how they would feel to know that they were, potentially, only referred to you because the person referring them to you was going to make a commission. That is called sales. That is not a referral. That is not a buddy or colleague helping them with a problem; it's **a person making a buck off their problem or pain**.

The trust established between the person being referred and the referral source has been lost and your potential new client is now not happy with you. Why? Because you paid for their business, and to make matters worse they now will question your competence to help them. Even if you are the best person to help them, confidence and trust have been destroyed and can be nearly impossible to re-create.

I know that you have probably been told that in order to make money, get business, you have to spend money, but paying for referrals is a very bad idea. It never ends well. You don't have to ask or pay for referrals to receive them. In fact, you can eliminate both of those strategies from your business development process.

A note about strategic alliances. Sometimes in certain businesses it's customary to pay for referrals received. In the online world, these alliances are referred to affiliates or joint venture partners. In the real estate world, a commission is paid if a licensed realtor refers a home buyer or seller to another licensed realtor. In addition to this being a customary and accepted business practice, it is also disclosed. The affiliate or commission relationship must be disclosed in advance to be part of the accepted business practice. When I talk about not paying for referrals I mean specifically the ones where the payment of commission is not disclosed. In my business—my online program—when I receive a new prospect through an affiliate or joint venture partnership I do not count that new prospect as a referral but as an affiliate lead. I believe when you pay for it, it is no longer a referral.

But asking and paying for referrals isn't the only reason why you may not be able to generate or receive them. Let's look at the other reasons you may not receive referrals.

Chapter
Five

OTHER REASONS WHY YOU MAY NOT RECEIVE REFERRALS

There are some recurring reasons I see that keep people from receiving referrals. The big one, as you now know, is asking for referrals, which prematurely cuts off the potential for getting them. But there are a few other reasons, possible roadblocks. When people approach me to talk about this problem I sometimes find myself having to be the bearer of two types of news. One is manageable for me to deliver, and I'm sure easier for them to receive because it has more to do with what they don't know that they need to be doing. The second type of news is bad news and is harder to deliver; it has to do with how they handle situations, there belief about how they should be "doing business."

Let's check to make sure you aren't getting in your own way when it comes to generating referrals. If you have put up barriers, you need to take them down. I'll give you some ideas on how to do that. First up are those reasons that are sometimes hard for me to deliver.

1. YOU MAKE IT ABOUT YOU.

You know the meeting: From the minute you sit down the other person just starts talking, and they only talk about themselves and they don't stop talking till the meeting is over. It comes across as self-centered because it is. Definitely avoid this behavior! If you only focus on you, why in the world would I care to help you? This self-centeredness probably doesn't just show up in coffee meetings. It may be that you lack self-awareness, or you truly believe you are owed something. If you make interactions about you, then more than likely that thinking will negatively impact how you approach receiving referrals. Remember, you aren't owed referrals even if you deserve them.

> REMEMBER, YOU AREN'T OWED REFERRALS EVEN IF YOU DESERVE THEM.

I watched this play out once after I gave a presentation on referrals. A person, we will call her Tina, approached me as I was talking to someone else from the audience. Tina launched into her story about how someone I know, we'll call her Margaret, has never given her a referral and should be giving her referrals. Tina's comments were entirely focused on herself. It was as if she couldn't see why Margaret may not be referring to her. She had an expectation of being owed referrals and her frustration was real, which she made loud and clear. Tina talked about how referrals from Margaret made sense because their businesses were complementary; she thought there must be something going on with Margaret for her not to refer her.

Yes, there was something going on with Margaret. My guess is that she was completely turned off by Tina and Tina's approach. Tina was making receiving referrals about her, and that violates why a referral would happen. In fact, the person I was talking to when Tina approached me to share her despair about Margaret said after Tina walked away, "I know Margaret, and I'm not surprised at all she isn't giving referrals to her."

Referrals aren't about you, so stop worrying that you aren't getting what you think you are owed. Start focusing on the other person in the equation, the potential referral source, and make their needs your priority. Then see if there is a shift in their actions towards you when it comes to helping you.

I also see this play out in networking meetings. There are a few I have been a part of that crack me up when I think back on them. They typically follow the same story line. Someone reaches out to you with a request to learn about your business, and you learn about their business. Or maybe their business has changed and they want to catch up. That is typically the language used when requesting a meeting; we would never agree to meet if they asked in advance to talk about themselves for an hour and show no interest in you. So you go to have coffee thinking you are going to learn about their business and share about your business. These are pure networking meetings, meaning there is supposed to be a give and take, a learning about each other. Sometimes, unfortunately, it seems there is only one person at the meeting. The person you meet with only focuses on making sure you know all about their business, their needs and how you can help them. They never stop to ask you about you, to understand how you are doing, or how they can help you. It is as if they forget you exist. And what makes those meetings the worst—other than the wasted hour you can never get back—is that they throw in a line at the end that is supposed to placate you. It goes something like this: "Now make sure you let me know how I can help you." Or if they do ask about you, it is within the final few minutes leaving you no time at all to have a meaningful conversation.

We must remember that nothing in life is all about us. Networking meetings definitely aren't. So please, if you are one of these people (I call them "one-siders"), stop doing all the talking, seriously. But it is not only that you do all the talking, it is that your mindset is focused on yourself and your needs only.

Curious if you are guilty of networking like this? There is an easy way to find out. If your networking meeting was because of an introduction by someone else, go back to the person who introduced you and ask them what the other person thought of you after meeting with you. If they are honest with you, they will share the truth, so give them permission to do just that. Don't get defensive, just take the feedback and learn from it.

Another way to help you adjust your mindset is to conduct your next twenty-five to fifty networking meetings 100 percent about the other person with no concern for yourself. Make those meetings about *them*. This will allow your mind-set to become more balanced in future meetings. Remember, we are always more inclined to help those who show they want to help us.

2. YOU AREN'T REFERRAL-WORTHY.

To receive referrals, you must be worthy. Period. One of two things could be preventing you from receiving referrals: either you deliver sub-par work, or your work is just average. Let's look at what it means to deliver sub-par work. Maybe you don't deliver sub-par work every time, but often enough to impact what your clients think about you; this does impact your referability. Now, no one is going to get everything right and you will have issues. But what I am referring to is that you consistently do inferior work (aka crappy work). Sorry. I know that isn't easy to hear. It may be because you haven't invested in the resources you need, or that you aren't effective and efficient with your time. Or you are overwhelmed and in over your head. Whatever the reason, you

TO RECEIVE REFERRALS, YOU MUST BE WORTHY. PERIOD.

don't deliver the quality of work your clients need to incline them to talk about you and refer others to you.

Doing sub-par work is easy to understand as a reason you wouldn't receive referrals, but so is average work. And by average work I mean that you do a good job but the overall experience with you from a client's perspective is one of being choppy. Choppy meaning that sometimes you shine: you deliver the work on time, and you communicate well. But sometimes you clearly miss the mark: no communication, late work with no explanation or you don't take ownership when things don't go well. You let the process run you instead of you running the process. If your client views your performance as choppy, then they'll see your product or service as average. And average work doesn't make an impression, nor is it memorable.

Here's the connection you have to make. Let's say I want to refer you one of my friends, colleagues or clients. The reason I want to refer you is because I know someone I care about who has a need or problem, and I want to make sure they're taken care of. If they receive a great client experience from you and speak highly of you, then I know I was helpful to them. Meaning that I played a part in making a difference for them. Let's be honest, that makes me feel like a hero. But to be the hero I need for you to provide an exceptional client experience; I want my friend, client, or colleague to get the best experience from start to finish. Not average. So if their client experience with you is choppy, it doesn't make an impression and I'm not willing to put my reputation on the line and refer you someone I care about.

What does "choppy" mean? Here are some examples:

- There are no expectations as to what I should expect as a client of yours. I am left to assume why things feel like they are taking too long or something doesn't go how I thought it would. As the client, it is never a good thing when I am left to assume.
- The communication from you or your office is sporadic, delayed, or seems to be provided as an afterthought.
- When there is an issue it takes too long for you to resolve it, or you don't resolve it at all. And sometimes you don't take responsibility for the issue.

- Your follow through is all over the board, i.e. sometimes you answer right away and sometimes there's a long delay.
- You were available for my every need during the "sales" process, but the minute I said yes to working with you and signed on the dotted line you disappeared.
- You have a team of people, but I don't know who to call when I need help.
- I've been a client for years, but I haven't heard from you in years.

Think about it. We may be willing to accept choppy service from a service provider we have committed to and started working with, but we will never connect someone we care about with a company that we know doesn't deliver. If your client experience is choppy, you leave a small piece of doubt in your client's mind, you don't make much of an impression, you lack a WOW and I won't be referring people to you.

But you can fix this. Focus on creating a repeatable process that all clients can experience, and if you have a team make sure they are on board with following the process. To do this sit down and list all the "steps" or touch points a client goes through from the point they say "Yes, I want to work with you" till the work is done. Think about the experience from a new client's perspective and from a client's perspective who has been with you for more than a year (the long-time client). Look for gaps or for places where you can up-level a process or add a wow. Nothing stops the flow of referrals faster than not being referral worthy.

At the end of this chapter look for the download section and grab the "What It Is Like To Work With You" Assessment. You will be able to answer a few simple questions about your client experience and rate how you are doing.

3. YOU LACK AUTHENTICITY.

When you care about the work you do and know why you do what you do, that shows through, both in you and in how your run your business (or manage your book of business). I have a strong and direct delivery mixed in with some sarcasm. But I care deeply. I believe my passion for and experience with generating referrals, plus caring that others have success, allows people to connect with me. I believe those that are drawn in to working with me get a sense of who I am—the real me, fully authentic, what you see is what you get. That doesn't mean I am for everyone though. In fact, that is a good thing.

You don't need to be like me to be authentic; in fact acting like me would be inauthentic for you. You need to be comfortable being authentic. Some people are introverts, some are extroverts, others cuss, and some don't. Some people have high, constant energy and others are more reserved and conscientious. Amanda, the personal injury attorney you learned about earlier, is more of an introvert, but that doesn't mean she doesn't develop relationships and carry on conversations that allow her to connect with her referral sources in a meaningful way.

Whatever you do, don't be fake. Remember, as businesses that must build relationships with prospects before they will become our clients, they are choosing us, not a company or brand. Trust and relationships really matter; we buy from humans. When I choose to work with you, I want to know I am getting an authentic version of who you are.

Now, the final two reasons you don't receive referrals are easier to deliver because they have more to do with not knowing what you should be doing; once you do know, you can easily fix the issues.

4. YOU LACK A PROCESS TO TAKE CARE OF YOUR REFERRAL SOURCES.

Before you can take care of your referral sources, you have to know who they are. If you don't know who your referral sources are, there is detailed information coming up in Chapter 8 to help you. But while knowing who your referral sources are is important, knowing what to do with them to cultivate ongoing referrals is also important.

You need a process, a plan you follow to strengthen relationships with your referral sources, so you can generate referrals. This just isn't any plan where you make sure you touch base twice a year or grab coffee occasionally. Because a system that reminds you to just reach out will only get you so far; simply keeping in touch isn't the same as making sure you're top of mind. You need a process, a plan to stay top of mind with your referrals sources and to stay top of mind you need to be memorable and meaningful. Which leads us to the other part you need to know to be in a position to receive referrals.

5. YOU FOCUS ON STAYING IN TOUCH, BUT YOU NEED TO BE TOP OF MIND.

When you shoot me an email to say hi or quickly say "hey" to me when you see me at a networking event, you are momentarily keeping in touch. Nothing wrong with that, but I only momentarily remember you. Because life is full of noise, and for most life moves quickly. For some relationships, like the many in your network, that is all you need. Being momentarily in touch is enough. But for my referral sources, if I am only momentarily remembered that won't generate additional referrals for me—three months or three years down the road.

When it comes to my referral sources I want to rise above the noise, rise above being remembered only in the moment, and make sure I am staying top of mind. You may think "staying in touch" and "staying top of mind" are just semantics. But they are not. To stay top of mind you must be memorable and meaningful. I believe staying top of mind creates a different mindset when it comes to how I act with and towards my referrals sources. When I reach out to my referral sources I want it to matter, by showing my gratitude for their referrals, by acknowledging what they mean to me, by letting them know I care about their business and how they are doing. I want them to connect with me on a level that means something to them and is memorable for them because they deserve it.

Sometimes we don't receive referrals because of our mindset: we are too focused on ourselves to deserve them, we don't provide a client experience worth talking about and we lack authenticity. But other times it's because we don't know there's something we need to be doing to generate referrals. I see many people get stuck in the trap of thinking certain tools are the answer, but what they are lacking is a comprehensive process to take care of their referral sources. Let's look at the tools people assume are all they need for their referral solution. Then we will unpack the five steps to creating a plan to generate referrals for your business.

<u>Chapter Download:</u>
What It Is Like To Work With You Assessment
To download please visit:
www.generatingbusinessreferrals.com/resources

Chapter Six

"TOOLS" ALONE AREN'T THE SOLUTION

Generating referrals is not a new topic for how to grow a business. In Chapter 3 we looked at many of the books written and the advice given on how to generate referrals. As you know, the majority of that advice centers around asking for referrals and keeping in touch with your network to generate referrals. But we know that keeping in touch doesn't equate to building a relationship with a referral source, and unless we have a relationship with them, we aren't going to receive ongoing referrals from them.

We must rise above the "keeping in touch" noise with outreach that matters…so we can stay top of mind. The problem is many people go looking for the easiest—and sometimes laziest—way to do outreach to their referrals sources in addition to their clients and network. Typically, we associate technology with "easy." We have the machine or robot or software do it for us so we don't have to.

This quest for "easiest" has allowed many services to pop up over the years. But easy doesn't mean slam dunk in terms of having an impact. And what typically happens when you find any easy way of doing something is that you begin to believe it's the entire solution: you begin to believe you only need that one "tool to generate the results you want.

But individual tools aren't the solution. In the final chapter of this book (Chapter 10) we are going to uncover the five steps you need to take to create a referral generating plan, to ensure you have referral success in your business. But before I can teach you those five steps and how to apply them in your business, we need to discuss how you may possibly view current tools as the solution.

Think of your referral generating plan as the toolbox, and remember to accomplish any task you need a fully stocked

> THINK OF YOUR REFERRAL GENERATING PLAN AS THE TOOLBOX, AND REMEMBER TO ACCOMPLISH ANY TASK YOU NEED A FULLY STOCKED TOOLBOX.

toolbox. But to generate the results you want you need to make sure you know when to use each tool and what results you can expect from each tool. Any one tool by itself isn't typically the solution, as one tool usually can't do the job by itself. Some tools are used more, like a hammer or screwdriver, because they are the main tools. Then some tools serve a more supporting role, like the level. And to be honest some tools you buy and then never actually end up using because they run counter to the results you desire. When we use individual tools to increase our referrals as the solution by themselves, separate from a complete referral generating plan toolbox, we run the risk of limiting our success; we fall into the trap of just keeping in touch because it's easier.

In my discussions with business owners and sales professionals I find many who use individual third-party managed products or SAAS (software as a service) programs as their only "tool" for generating referrals. Others believe that membership in referral or lead groups is all they need. And some believe that the marketing they are currently doing is serving their referral needs, so they don't need to do anything additional. I'm not going to break down the pros and cons of individual tools but do want to address how and why they aren't the solution, particularly if you are looking for a complete referral generating plan (aka your referral toolbox).

THIRD-PARTY MANAGED PRODUCTS

The most commonly used third-party product is cards you send out to keep in touch with your clients, prospects and network. Examples of companies that will send out a card, so you don't have to, include Send Out Cards™, Handwrytten, Bond, Handiemail, and Inkly. They allow you to have someone else (or a machine or robot) send out a card from you. The argument is it is faster and easier. But it is faking a card from you; this is particularly true with the services that try to mimic your handwriting.

Most of these products offer an application (app) to use to order your cards so that it is fast and easy. This is a top selling point as to why you would use the service. But if you want impact—to stay top of mind—then you may need to be willing to forgo the "easy" way and focus on the most impactful way. Remember, most robotic-sent cards are quickly thrown in the trash because there's no value associated with them. You get the exact opposite reaction when you send a handwritten card. The most impactful way is to show your referral source how much they mean to you because you are willing to sit down with pen and paper and write them a note to express your gratitude. That takes time—in all honesty, just a few minutes really— and when we do something that takes time it is recognized by others because unfortunately it is not done that often. So it is not that you sent a card, it is that you took your precious time to put thoughts to pen and paper in your own handwriting. We all recognize that time is our most precious commodity, and when we are willing to take our time for someone else—in this case our referral source—and not "cheat" in the process, we are rewarded by being top of mind.

It is the same thing with eCards (emailed cards). While some of those are funny (jib jab, anyone?), it isn't lost on anyone that it is easier to send an eCard than a card you wrote yourself. I do think a third-party managed option can have its place in your toolbox, but it shouldn't be the only tool or even an often-used tool. It is a supporting tool and should be used accordingly.

SAAS (SOFTWARE AS A SERVICE)

Another option that has been around for at least the last 10 years is to consider using a software program to help you promote yourself as you try to gather referrals. Companies who sell these programs include Referral Key, Refer.com, Alignable, and Treble. The idea behind these SAAS companies is to leverage technology to grow businesses by using the internet and creating an online community to allow people to refer each other. While in theory the concept sounds great, if we apply what a referral really is to these concepts, it is effectively "passing" leads. You need to fill out a profile and then sometimes connect with your current network to get the process going. So this becomes a way to promote your business but this doesn't mean it will create referral sources you can count on. Now, some of the SAAS services go further than just an online community to connect to receive referrals, but they are only as good as the information you provide and the other people you know who are committed to using it.

So you may use one of the third-party managed products or SAAS products to augment or complement your referral generating plan, but they cannot be *the plan* because you are shortchanging the referral success you could be having. Another way people focus on only one tool for generating referrals is to believe that a leads group (though called a referral group) or networking group will supply them a steady stream of referrals.

LEADS AND NETWORKING GROUPS

Ultimately these groups want (or should want) to deliver opportunities to allow their members to foster relationships.

That's when these types of groups hit their mark. But they can only be as successful as the members allow them to be. Belonging to one or a dozen groups isn't necessarily a recipe for referral success. Also, having a rule or perceived as having a rule about mandatory "referrals" can impact success as well. Because when you force referrals—make it mandatory or part of how members are ranked—then it isn't about developing relationships and helping people who have a need identified; instead it becomes about passing leads. The focus becomes more about scrolling through your contacts to find a few names before the next meeting in order to meet a written or unwritten requirement. And as you learned in Chapter 2 a warm lead is not a referral, no matter how badly we wish it was.

There are a few types or categories of groups and they range on a spectrum in terms of structure, expectations of their members and the objective of the group. Some will refer to themselves as a leads group, a networking group or a referral group. I am always cautious when I see a group presenting itself as a referral group since you cannot manufacture referrals. The spectrum also ranges from groups that are national or regional with a set structure for how meetings and leads ("referrals") are to be handled. Then, on the other end of the spectrum there are organizations that hope to provide networking and educational opportunities for members that may result in members doing business with each other or referring each other. (See Figure B.)

TYPE OF GROUPS	STRUCTURE	EXAMPLES
National and Regional Leads Groups	Highly structured but operate at the local level – like a franchise model, dues, weekly meetings, mandatory attendance	BNI, WIN, Caersunet
Local Lead Groups	Can be highly structured but they create their own rules, may or may not have dues monthly or weekly meetings	Locally Named
Networking Associations	Focus on networking and education opportunities, different monthly meetings depending on topic, Mastermind offerings, usually do not have mandatory attendance	Chambers of Commerce, NAWBO chapters (National Association of Women Business Owners), EO (Entrepreneurs Associations)

Figure B

It would be unfair to compare the different groups without being able to do so comprehensively, but here are a few flags to look out for. For the structured national, regional and even local groups, is your attendance mandatory? If so, why is it mandatory? If it is because you have to pass out so many names of people/prospects to members in the group (leads), then you should be concerned. If attendance is mandatory (or there is an attendance policy) to make sure you are committed to the group, then that makes sense since your attendance is needed to be able to foster relationships with people in the group. But don't just use the weekly or monthly structured meetings to get to know other members; meet up for one-on-ones and get involved in getting to know the members. Members of groups like this can become future COI (centers of influence) referral sources, but like referrals it takes time for someone to develop into a COI; that process can't be forced or rushed. You need to allow time for the relationships to develop.

AUTOMATED NEWSLETTER

It really amazes me how many times I ask someone how they stay top of mind with their referral sources and the answer I receive is, "I have an automated monthly newsletter I send out to my database." My first red flag is that they consider reaching out to their database to be the same thing as reaching out to their referral sources (but of course you know better because you are reading this book). As you can imagine, I question if they even know who their referral sources are. I'm also worried that they believe their automated marketing newsletter (emailed or mailed) is a worthy substitute for staying top of mind and building relationships with their referral sources.

I'm not saying you shouldn't have a monthly newsletter, as they serve a purpose within your marketing plan. The goal of a marketing newsletter is to keep the brand in front of your prospects and clients, to educate them and typically to include something sales related. But outreach to a referral source is on an entirely different level. We are building a relationship with them, not trying to market to them. We need to have an entire outreach plan, a referral generating plan (the whole toolbox), when it comes to taking care of our referral sources. You can include your referral sources on the distribution list for your company newsletter, but you need to be following a true referral generating plan where you use other outreach to reach the top of mind status. The marketing newsletter won't offend your referral sources, but to generate referrals from them we need to do more than just mass distribution outreach. The problem I find that some people use the newsletter as their only tool, and if your referral sources are only hearing from you when you are pitching or just "keeping in touch" via your newsletter, you aren't cultivating relationships with them.

Relationship cultivation is at the heart of a referral generating plan, so let's dive in deeper to understanding what that looks like and how you can generate referrals without asking.

RELATIONSHIP CULTIVATION IS AT THE HEART OF A REFERRAL GENERATING PLAN

Chapter
Seven

BEYOND ASKING:
FIVE STEPS TO GENERATE REFERRALS

If you have made it this far in the book, then you had an opportunity to go deeper with your understanding of how to generate referrals. This includes:

- Understanding the difference between a warm lead, an introduction, word of mouth buzz and a referral.
- Knowing the three players or cast of characters in the referral process and being very clear on each players' role.
- Being well versed in why asking and paying for referrals is wrong, and how those tactics can damage your future ability to receive referrals.
- Being clear on the other reasons why you may not be receiving referrals, from making conversations all

about you or just focusing on keeping in touch and never making it to top of mind status.

- Understanding how some third-party tools—though they sell themselves as whole packages to generate referrals—are tools that can only augment your referral strategy, and knowing you have to use them correctly, some only sparingly.

- Most importantly you are now able to see your referral sources in a whole new light—as the heroes they are— and know you need to up your game to continually treat them right in order to stay top of mind.

The next legitimate question is "What's next?" How do you take your ability to generate referrals to the next level so you can grow and sustain your business through referrals? Coming up you will learn tactics to not only identify but increase your number of referral sources, the exact language to plant referral seeds so you never have to ask, and you'll learn how to build a referral generating plan that can sustain long-term referral growth.

You'll learn more about Amanda, the personal injury attorney who transformed her business by sustaining referral growth for multiple years and counting. I'm not talking about having one good quarter, or even one good year, of referral generation. I'm talking about the ability to grow your referrals in a sustainable way to become your top client-generating strategy, to know your business can count on referrals month in and month out, year in and year out.

What you need is a referral generating plan. A referral generating plan is similar to having a sales or prospecting plan and a marketing plan; a referral generating plan stands on it own. It's a separate plan you follow to increase your referrals from existing referral sources or to develop and cultivate new referral sources. Let me define each of the plans so you can see how the referral plan is different from the prospecting plan or marketing plan.

THREE-PLAN BREAKDOWN

PROSPECTING PLAN:

This is the plan you need if you "want to eat tomorrow." The plan entails activities done in hopes of creating short-term success. For example, heading to the networking event where you hope to meet one or two prospects who will agree to meet for coffee to discuss the possibility of working together. This is the "pound the pavement or phones" type of plan that can produce results but takes a huge commitment of ongoing and consistent activity. You can be less reliant on this plan once you have an established referral plan.

MARKETING/BRANDING PLAN:

This plan helps you establish yourself in the marketplace and build credibility. Depending on your budget it may just include an online presence with a website and a few social media accounts. A more robust budget may include advertising (online and print) or earned media through publicity. You will also need some version of this plan to maintain credibility or name recognition in the marketplace. Note: If you work for a company or corporation this part of the overall sales strategy may already be determined for you.

REFERRAL PLAN:

This is the ultimate plan, where new clients come to you through referrals, where new clients show up in your inbox because someone connected them to you knowing you can help solve the client's problem. Now, growing a sustainable and consistent referral plan doesn't happen overnight, but following the right steps outlined in the following chapters can produce consistent results where you can hit your yearly new client or sales goals from referrals. This allows you to lessen your reliance on a prospecting plan or marketing/branding plan. My goal for you is to eliminate as much activity from your prospecting plan as possible because you are experiencing consistent results with referrals. Sound good?

It is important to remember that any referrals I receive wouldn't show up if I didn't provide value, if I didn't do great work, and if I wasn't referable. But the referrals also wouldn't show up if I didn't take care of my referral sources by showing them the gratitude they deserve, continually strengthened my relationship with them and made a commitment to be meaningful and memorable so I stay top of mind. Developing a strong base of referral sources—so I can

CREATING A REFERRAL GENERATING PLAN SHOULDN'T BE COMPLICATED.

cultivate ongoing referrals from those sources—means I need to follow a plan and act on that plan.

Let's dive into what the referral generating plan looks like. The good news is that creating a referral generating plan shouldn't be complicated. There is some work involved to create and execute the plan, but following a referral plan beats cold calling, incessant networking or stalking on LinkedIn any day of the week.

There are five basic steps you need to take to create a business that is sustained by referrals. But remember, as you've learned throughout this book, these five steps are built with the understanding that you do great work and are worthy of referrals. Think of being referable as the foundation and the five steps move you up from the foundation to generating consistent referrals that sustain your business growth. Let's look at each step in detail through the next few chapters.

FIVE STEPS TO CREATING A REFERRAL GENERATING PLAN

1. Identify who refers you or should be referring you, your referral sources.
2. Master an immediate thank-you process.
3. Build for the long term, execute in the short term.
4. Plant the right referral seeds.
5. Automate the plan and measure results.

Before we unpack each of the five steps, just remember the goal of this book is to give you a plan to follow so you control your referral generation and keeps you out of the "always be asking for referrals" club. But even when you have a roadmap to follow, there is work involved. So if you are up for some work—highly enjoyable work though—then let's dive in. And in the process, let's leave the "always be asking" club and its first cousin the "always be closing" club behind and join a different group, the "always generating referrals" club. Welcome and here we go!

LET'S LEAVE THE "ALWAYS BE ASKING" CLUB AND ITS FIRST COUSIN THE "ALWAYS BE CLOSING" CLUB BEHIND AND JOIN A DIFFERENT GROUP, THE "ALWAYS GENERATING REFERRALS" CLUB

Chapter Download:
5 Steps to a Referral Generating Plan Cheat Sheet
To download please visit:
www.generatingbusinessreferrals.com/resources

Chapter Eight

STEP ONE:
IDENTIFY YOUR REFERRAL SOURCES

Knowing who refers to you is the most important step in generating referrals. You have to know who your referral sources are (aka your heroes). The easiest place to start is by looking at where your current or past clients came from, meaning how did they find out about you. If you have a sense that you have no referral sources, don't worry. There's information coming up on how to increase your referral sources. But I still want you to go through this process, just to be sure.

IDENTIFYING YOUR HEROES

You need to be crystal clear on who refers to you by knowing exactly who your referral sources are, as in knowing them by name. The easiest way to get a handle on who your referral sources are is to look back at your previous clients and determine how they came to you. How did they first learn about you? If you can gather the sources of your clients for the past two to three years you are on a clear path to creating your list of referral sources. The best way to do this is to sit down with a list of your clients; go back as many years back as you can. Looking back two or three years will give you good data, but if you have been in business for, say, ten years, then go back at least five years. Gold star for you if you go back all ten years, or for however long you have been in business. I have had students

> YOU NEED TO BE CRYSTAL CLEAR ON WHO REFERS TO YOU BY KNOWING EXACTLY WHO YOUR REFERRAL SOURCES ARE, AS IN KNOWING THEM BY NAME.

in my online program who have been in business for ten to fifteen-plus years take the time to pull as much of their client data as possible. So I'm sure you can too. Keep in mind, you may be able to pull this information from a CRM tool (client relationship management tool) or you'll do it the old-fashioned way with pen and paper.

Let's look at what client data you will pull and the method you'll use.

GETTING TO THE RIGHT SOURCE

There are a lot of sources or ways for a client to become a client. The word "source" means how the client heard about you. There are many different types of sources including but not limited to:

- Attending a networking event
- Meeting you at a trade show
- Finding you in an online search like Google or an online advertisement
- Seeing your sponsorship of an event or charity
- Approaching you after seeing you give a presentation
- Answering a printed advertisement
- Reading an article you wrote in a trade publication
- Receiving direct mail from you
- Answering one of your cold calls or cold emails
- And the best kind of source—a referral from someone

Don't include clients who became your clients because of an acquisition of another business or a book of business.

PULLING THE DATA USING A CRM TOOL

If you use a CRM (client relationship management tool) you should be able to generate a report that lists your clients and the sources. If you have the capability to pull those clients with the date they became clients please do so; it will make the data even richer for you.

Keep in mind that you will only be able to pull the client list with the sources attached if you entered that information. Almost all CRMs have a "source" field but you still had to *complete* that field any time you entered a new client or prospect; otherwise the information won't magically be there. If you didn't enter the information, then pull your list of clients and move on to the second way of identifying your referral sources: with pen, paper and your memory.

PULLING THE DATA USING PEN AND PAPER

If you don't have a CRM or don't have this information captured somewhere else (like in an Excel document) you can follow the second way to generate the list of those who refer you. Consider it a necessary walk down memory lane. You will need to create a list of your clients and sit down with that list and try to remember how they first heard about you. Sometimes you'll remember where your clients came from, and other times you may be able to look in their files, review notes you took during your first prospect meeting with them, scan emails you sent, or check any notes you may have collected in your calendar, etc. Now this second way definitely takes longer, but trust me it will be totally worth it.

HOW FAR BACK?

A question I receive all the time is "How far back do I have to go?" Meaning, how many years of clients do I need to pull to have a good representation of your referral sources? Now I mentioned earlier that you should at least go back two to three years or half the time you have been in business. But regardless, you need to pull a list of clients that goes back at least two years. Also, you may find that clients referred to you ten years ago do not match your current ideal client, meaning you'll need to consider if the referral sources—those people who referred you those clients ten years ago—are still relevant and will make your final referral source list. And remember, I have had students go back five, ten or more years and some are able to go back all the way to when they started their businesses. Virtual fist bump to those people.

DO I INCLUDE ONLY CLIENTS?

An additional step you can take that will make this client source data richer and tell a more complete picture is to include prospects you received through any source but who didn't become clients. Why is this important? Because a referral source is a referral source even if the prospect they referred to you didn't become a client. For our purposes, as we create our first list of referral sources, the outcome doesn't matter. What matters is that a referral source thought enough of you to refer someone to you. You won't ever have a 100 percent close ratio on every referred prospective client, so you'll need your list of hero referral sources to include everyone who refers or has referred to you.

I do recognize that this information is harder to capture than just creating a list of clients. Your clients are your clients; of course you know them or know how to pull the information to create the list. You might have only met a prospect once, but if you can re-create this list of prospects your list of referral sources will be stronger and richer. One tip on how to re-create this list is to do a review of your calendar and make a list of the prospects you met. (I color code my prospect meetings in dark green, so it does make it easier to "see" all my prospect meetings at a glance.) Once you have the prospects written down you can check your emails or files by searching for the prospect's name to see if you captured any information on how they heard about you, found you or you found them.

FINALIZING THE LIST

Now remember, once you have your list you are just going to focus on those clients or prospects who came through referral sources. Essentially, just remove all clients and their sources if the sources were not referrals. After removing all "non-referral" sources you will be left with a list of your heroes and the clients or prospects they referred to you. Keep this list; you don't ever want to have to re-create it. And coming up I'll teach you how to build on the list by tracking upcoming referrals received.

Keep in mind, this step takes the most work of all five steps and if you do it right it will be hugely beneficial to you in many ways. (For a step-by-step guide to this process see the Chapter Download section at the end of this chapter.)

UNCOVERING HIDDEN DATA IN YOUR BUSINESS

For my Growth By Referrals online and VIP students, I provide a "Client Look Back" document that helps makes this process more manageable. It gives them a step-by-step guide to list their clients and capture, as best they can, their referral sources. But the processes outlined above for pulling this information together will help you get what you need. Just don't forget to include prospects and their sources, and go back as far as you can.

Completing step one in our five-step process is excellent data for your business and provides you with a necessary starting point. In addition, you will know the following important data points after you complete step one. You will know:

- Who has actually referred to you (this may surprise you)
- How many times they have referred you (the farther you go back in years the better)
- The type of prospective new client they referred to you (important later if you want to change the type of referrals you receive)
- An overview of your close ratio by referral source (you'll be able to determine how well you close—turn a prospect into a client—with those referred to you by each source)

But you can also use this data for much more. Consider this tip.

PRO TIP: I want to give you a smart move you should consider regarding what to do with the other source data you have collected during this process. And by the other data I mean those clients who came to you through other sources, non-referral sources, like advertisements, networking events, cold calls, your website, etc. This data is helpful because it will show you the other client generation strategies that are working or not working in your business. For example, if you spent a lot of money on print advertising and all your clients from the past three years came through referrals, social media advertising and speaking engagements, then you now can make an informed decision as to whether you need to continue to spend your time and money on the print advertising efforts. The goal is to identify which client generation techniques are working and which are not and then eliminating those not working. Having definitive data helps you make smarter business decisions as to where you spend your money.

CONSIDERATIONS AFTER COMPLETING STEP ONE

Typically, two concerns are raised after completing this exercise. The first is, what if you don't have two years or more of clients to look back through? Meaning, if your business is new you won't have many— or any—referral sources. The second concern is, what if you pull the data for the last five years (or more) and the smallest source of all your new clients is referral sources? Meaning, most of your new clients or prospects have come through other means and were not referred to you. It is okay; don't stress.

At least half of the businesses I work with start in this place. I call it *starting from scratch*. When you go through your clients and prospects to pull out the sources you may not have enough sources or any. Which means you will need to first focus on growing your base of referral sources. It works the same way if you are new in business or just don't have many clients yet; you simply don't have many sources, including referral sources.

It is important at this point to identify who should be referring you. Referrals, as you have learned, typically come from two main places: clients and centers of influence (COI).

Most people want a combination of both clients and COI, but some people only have one type. There is not a right or wrong way; it is more about what will work within your business.

Let's look at the steps to take to increase your referrals sources if you don't have enough or even any. I also encourage you to download the "Increasing Your COI Referral Sources" activity to help you during this process. You can learn how to download it in the resource section of this book. The exercise is a great place to start to identify your ideal referral sources, so you can build the foundation to cultivate them.

DEVELOPING MORE HEROES

How do you get more referral sources, or more heroes? This isn't an issue that only concerns those who don't start with many referral sources. Even when you have a larger list of referrals sources that is more developed, most people find themselves wanting to develop more. There is a fluid quality to the list and the reality is that someone who was on the list two years ago might not be on it two years from now. Some will never fall off the list and some will. That is normal. People move, retire, change jobs or sell their businesses; therefore, their ability to refer you new clients diminishes or in some cases just ends.

The basic advice I always give on how to develop more referral sources is to first know who makes the ideal referral source for you. They will have one of the following traits in common (possibly multiple traits). These aren't in any particular order.

1. They need you as a resource for their clients. For example, a financial advisor needs a CPA to recommend to his clients regarding tax strategies and management of tax burdens. Or a home builder needs an architect, drafter and interior designer to recommend to his clients because without house plans, drawings or design the builder cannot provide a cost estimate. For another example, a realtor needs a quality mortgage broker and home inspector because a house cannot be purchased without both.

2. They are well connected. They are what I call "natural connectors." Many of my COI are well connected, which increases the number of people they will come in contact with who may need my services. Connectors can't help but connect people to each other; it is almost as if they thrive on it and it's a fantastic part of who they are. You know you've met one because during the course of your conversation they come up with at least two to three people they want to introduce you to. It's not always potential clients but people you may need to know.

3. They are clients who are raving fans. They often give you rave reviews. They are gold because they know intimately what it is like to work with you; they only speak from experience, which most people prefer when seeking a recommendation. But what makes these clients special is that they are willing to talk about you and aren't shy about making a connection when they know someone who needs your service.

Once you have an idea of who makes the best referral sources, then you need to create a list or profile of who you are looking for. Do you need more clients to refer to you? Or do you need more COI? Or both? Consider looking at your list of clients and determine if some of them are connectors, which means you need to do a better job of nurturing your relationships with them. If you need more COI referral sources, then consider who they are. For example, if you are a drafter who draws up home designs, then you might need more home builders to refer you drafting work. But sometimes you aren't clear on exactly who you need as a referral source; you just know the qualities you are looking for in an ideal referral source.

You need to be intentional about growing your list of referral sources. It is easier when it is clients because they are more easily identified, but don't overlook the importance of growing your COI. You'll do more one-on-one networking in search of a few good COI. The time this takes will be worth it. For those you meet who do not turn out to be good COI, they can stay within your network, but you won't need to actively pursue building stronger relationships with them.

I mentioned at the beginning of Chapter 7 my client Amanda, the personal injury attorney. When we started working together toward the end of 2014 she was receiving around six to seven referrals a year from one partner within her firm. The concern was that she wanted to expand her practice, and she knew that partner would eventually retire. She wanted to be ready for the day his referrals ended.

When we went through the process to develop her list of referral sources, we quickly identified that if we wanted to increase her referrals we would have to increase her referral sources; the focus would need to be COI, not clients, due to the nature of her work. We worked to identify who her ideal COIs would be and then created a list. It was slow at first and she had to push through being an introvert; she needed to be willing to meet different people.

By the end of 2014 Amanda's number of referrals sources was slowly growing; she was up to twelve referrals received. In 2015, she received twenty-seven referrals, more than doubling her referrals over the previous year. And the referrals just kept growing. In 2016 she hit thirty new referrals, and in 2017, she was on pace to hit thirty new referrals again. In 2018, she fully expects to reach her yearly target of twenty-five to thirty new referrals for the fourth year in a row.

What is fascinating about Amanda's referral growth is that it all started with her willingness to do the work involved. As an attorney, she only needs around twelve cases a year to fill her workload, so with her bringing in more than double that she has been able to pick and choose the cases she takes. This has provided a new feeling of freedom for her. In addition, she was able to hire an additional attorney, allowing her team to grow and to have a partner to work on cases with. To get you started with the same process Amanda went through, see the free download "Increasing Your COI Referral Sources" in the resource section.

You can never underestimate the importance of your referral sources (clients and COI) because your livelihood depends on them. You may not feel that way now if you aren't receiving many referrals. But once the majority of your prospective new clients come through referrals versus the other tactics you used to use (in my case a lot of networking and free speaking), you will be able to recognize the power of your referrals sources and why they are so important to your business growth and sustainability. Take a good look at your referral sources—the heroes. Those heroes are GOLD to your business, no

THOSE HEROES ARE GOLD TO YOUR BUSINESS, NO MATTER HOW BIG OR HOW SMALL YOUR LIST IS

matter how big or how small your list is. Later on, we'll discuss how you take care of them in an ongoing way.

Chapter Downloads:
Id Your Referral Sources Checklist
Increasing Your COI Referral Sources Activity
To download please visit:
www.generatingbusinessreferrals.com/resources

Chapter Nine

STEP TWO:
MASTER YOUR IMMEDIATE FOLLOW-UP PROCESS

S tep two in our process is sometimes easily overlooked or rushed through because it seems extremely obvious. But all five steps build on each other and you cannot move on to step three until you have this one mastered. The immediate thank-you process consists of two steps:

1. Tracking the referrals received
2. Sending thank-you cards

TRACKING REFERRALS

Let's first tackle the referral tracker. When it comes to tracking your referrals received, you just need a few data points to collect. When we try to track too much data it starts to overwhelm us, and we are more likely to abandon it. Tracking referrals should be easy, one of the easiest processes you have in your business.

You need to have one document where you capture some basic information: the date the referral was received, the name of the referral source and the name of the prospect (prospective new client) they referred to you. You can also track outcome— if they become a client or not—although when you're getting started this is optional. There is no need to complicate this step; in the resource section for this book you can download my referral tracker for free. It is super simple and basic…very basic…just an Excel document with a few columns and rows. Simple but powerful, I promise.

Once you have the referral tracker, you need a "keeper" of the tracker. If you are a solopreneur then you are the keeper. I was for many years. But if you have an assistant—virtual or local; part-time or full-time—you can delegate the job of "keeper" to them. It doesn't matter who the keeper is; it's just important to have someone responsible for the list.

USING AN ASSISTANT TO TRACK REFERRALS

Here is how my assistant and I follow the referral capture process. When someone refers me to another person—a prospective client—I simply send the information to my virtual assistant (VA) and she inputs the data in the tracker. We track the date, the referral source's name,

BY TRACKING YOU ARE GUARANTEED TO NEVER LOSE A REFERRAL; NO REFERRAL LEFT BEHIND!

and the prospect's name. Boom! That's it. Pretty simple, right? She loads the information in and then can send me the most up-to-date version of the tracker when I ask for it. Almost 100 percent of my referrals come through email because that is how I position myself to receive them. Which means that capturing them and being in the driver's seat to follow up is much easier.

Following this process, I can feel confident that I will have a record of each referral received. There are many reasons to keep your referral tracker current:

- You know how many referrals you received in a month, quarter or year.
- You know who to thank because you keep track of your referral sources.
- You know how to categorize your referral sources to leverage more referrals (based on how many referrals received from any one referral source).
- You know who you should be following up with to become new clients.

Track every time, all the time. By tracking you are guaranteed to never lose a referral; no referral left behind!

THANK-YOU CARDS

I believe you should invest in note cards and stamps. Use those cards to write thank-you notes for past referrals, acknowledge what your referral sources means to your business, or just say hi and thinking about you. You can buy some inexpensive note cards from a local store or spend less than a hundred dollars to have cards printed with your logo. You may not have to pay a designer if you design the cards online just using your logo, but you'll always have to pay for printing. The only time I think it's okay to use your company logo as part of your referral process is on the thank you notes.

If you want to go a little further with your thank-you cards, I encourage you to create ones that are memorable or funny. When you can catch someone's attention, they are more likely to remember it. I designed a few different thank-you cards for my business and people appreciated receiving them. One of my favorite cards is my *Keep Calm and Referral On* thank- you card. It plants the "referral seed" right on the cover of the card with the use of the word "referral" on it.

Referral On Thank-You Card

I only use this card when thanking someone for sending me a referral because the cover of this card wouldn't make sense if I sent it to someone who hadn't referred me. You can download the *Referral On* thank-you card in the resource section of this book. Save yourself the designer fee and use my design; you'll just need to have them printed (and supply envelopes).

THE RIGHT THANK-YOU CARD LANGUAGE

Regardless of the design of the card, the real magic is what you write in the note. Below is the basic language to use on the card. Please note, you may have to change the language to fit your circumstances or make it sound like you. That's fine but stay as close to the language I provide as you can.

_____ (insert referral sources name),

"I just wanted to take a moment to thank you for the referral to _____ (insert the first and last name of the person they referred).

I am grateful for your support and trusting me to help the people you know and care about. Please let me know if I can do anything for you."

Your name

Now again, change the language as it fits you. You may want to get more personal or mention something specific in the note. But make sure to include the three basic parts of the card.

1. Thank for each referral received by name.
2. Let them know you appreciate the referral(s).

3. Offer to help them.

I encourage you to send out thank-you cards as soon as possible once a referral has been received. I believe one to two days is a great timeframe to aim for, but make sure you have the note in the mail before a week has gone by. To nail step two, you need to track your referrals and then send the appropriate thank-you note within a reasonable time period. And, truthfully, the sooner the better.

But just knowing what to say in a thank-you card when you receive a referral and tracking your referrals won't provide you the consistent, steady stream of referrals you need to truly grow your business. What you need is a fully functioning referral plan, as your outreach to referral sources in between receiving referrals is critical to increasing the number of referrals you will receive in the future.

<u>Chapter Downloads:</u>
Referral Tracker
Referral On Thank-You Card Design
(download a color version and a black & white version)
To download please visit:
www.generatingbusinessreferrals.com/resources.

Chapter Ten

STEP THREE:
BUILD FOR THE LONG TERM, EXECUTE IN THE SHORT TERM

What makes a referral generating plan so simple yet so crucial for your business is that it is *a plan*. One that you follow for it to work, of course, but you plan it out in advance. Well-known management consultant Brian Tracey's advice has withstood the test of time and is still critical today; *"For every minute spent in planning, it saves 10 minutes in execution."* For my Growth By Referrals online and VIP students, we build their referral generating plans on a 12-month cycle. This way we can see what we are going to do to build and strengthen our relationships with our referral sources and can assess the cost for an entire year. Now, a referral generating plan does not require a big budget; in fact, you can build your plan on a shoestring budget.

The length of time you build your plan for and your budget considerations are just logistics though. What makes this plan work is the outreach to your referral sources, called touch points. Your touch points are *what you are going to do,* and your referral sources are on the receiving end of this plan.

Remember, this all goes back to my referral philosophy that I shared at the beginning of the book.

Referrals only come from relationships.

Relationships come from connecting.

And connections are built through ongoing touch points.

The reason for the touch points, your outreach to your referral sources, is to keep you top of mind by being memorable and meaningful. Our goal is to create an ongoing experience for our referral sources that encourages them to send more referrals. While our referral sources will have an experience, for us to provide that experience we are just executing on the process that we built, our plan.

When building this plan, we must follow the 3 Platinum Principles™ of generating referrals. It is important we don't violate these three principles because they allow us to be authentic but keeps the focus on the hero, the referral source.

> **REFERRALS ONLY COME FROM RELATIONSHIPS. RELATIONSHIPS COME FROM CONNECTING. AND CONNECTIONS ARE BUILT THROUGH ONGOING TOUCH POINTS.**

3 PLATINUM PRINCIPLES™

1. Must be all about them
2. Must be authentic to you
3. Must keep you top of mind

Since referrals come from relationships, you must look at each of the three principles from that perspective. To receive more referrals, we need to be focused on developing deeper relationships with those who do refer us or could refer us. And by deeper relationships, I don't mean "let's grab a beer every night after work." What I mean is taking time to know your referral sources, understand what matters to them, what they need, and why they refer you.

The Platinum Principles guide the decisions you make when creating the experiences, the moments, the touch points for your referral sources. Let's look at each one in more detail.

PLATINUM PRINCIPLE #1: MUST BE ALL ABOUT THEM

You cannot confuse marketing, branding or promotion with referrals. While marketing, branding and promotion have their place within your business, they should not impact how you structure your referral plan.

When you think about your referral sources first consider what you can do that makes it all about them. What do they need? And, specifically, what do they need from you? Remember the number one reason someone refers to you isn't about you; it's about helping someone they know who has an issue that you just happen to be able to solve. But most of us do like to be thanked or acknowledged when we give a referral. So focus on what you can do that shows your gratitude. Think about what you can do to make the connection and relationship all about them—genuinely and authentically?

Can you share knowledge about your industry that will help one of your referral sources run their business smarter? Can you invite them to a business event where they can learn and network? Can you give them a gift that shows you know and understand their world? Like giving a parent or pet owner a car wash gift card to acknowledge them and what they mean to you. Most parents and pet owners would agree that an occasional car wash is always a good thing. But a word of caution, when giving gifts don't include your logo on them. For example, a water bottle with your logo just won't cut it for a referral acknowledgment. An item with your logo on it is actually all about you.

PLATINUM PRINCIPLE #2: MUST BE AUTHENTIC TO YOU

When considering and applying Platinum Principle #1, you must balance what they need against what feels authentic to you. Meaning don't include touch points that don't work for you or fit you as a part of your referral experience. This is probably best explained with an example or two.

I worked with a financial advisor on his referral plan, and when we started talking about what his referral sources needed (clients and COI) he was clear on Platinum Principle #1. He was extremely appreciative of his referrals sources, but there was a fundamental principle of who he is that he had to honor. To him it was more important to be a part of his kids' lives by throwing the ball in the front yard, coaching their sports teams and being home for dinner. Which means he wasn't interested in having to spend a lot of time after hours with his referral sources, like grabbing a beer, attending dinner charity events or networking dinners. Because what was most important to him was to head home after work and be a dad, spend time with his kids. It wasn't that his referral sources weren't important, it was just that being a dad was more important. So I would never create a plan for him that violated who he was as a person because he wouldn't have enjoyed it and it wouldn't have been authentic to him.

Using myself as an example, I happen to like to entertain (my poor husband). So for my clients and my referral sources I host a backyard movie event each fall. The event is a client appreciation party, but I also invite my referral sources who are not clients to attend to acknowledge what they mean to my business and to give them a night out with the family; all they have to do is show up and have fun. The language I use to invite my referral sources is important (keep reading for details on the language). To honor Platinum Principle #2, you must consider what is most authentic to you as you build your referral generating plan.

PLATINUM PRINCIPLE #3: MUST KEEP YOU TOP OF MIND

The final piece of the Platinum Principles is to create touch points, experiences, moments that keep you top of mind. What that means is you cannot do just one and consider your work done. A one-hit wonder touch point won't work, not in the long term; it won't produce the consistent referral results you are after. Touch points may be face to face like grabbing coffee, something you mail like a card, a gift you send, a business introduction or connection you make for a referral source, or an event you host. There are many different types of touch points as opportunities to create experiences, moments. The possibilities are endless. You just need to take some time to consider what your referral sources need and what you are willing to do. If you focus on your touch points being memorable and meaningful—I call it minding your M&Ms—you will have greater impact.

The reason we want to move past staying in touch and move to staying top of mind is because when we are top of mind, we build the habit in our referral sources of sending more prospective new clients our way. But to stay top of mind you cannot just send an email every few months with a "Hey, how you are?" note. Remember, you need to be memorable and meaningful.

BE MEMORABLE AND MEANINGFUL.

***

Use these 3 Platinum Principles™ to build your plan to deliver touch points that will have an impact on your referral sources. What you build should reflect who you are but be focused on what the referral sources need or want. But your referral generating plan needs a final piece before we move to putting it into action and measuring its results (Chapter 12). What you need next is to understand how to use the right language for the touch points you just created. That language is called referral planting seeds, and you will also need to be aware of other times to plant these seeds outside of your pre-planned touch points.

Chapter
Eleven

STEP FOUR:
PLANT THE RIGHT REFERRAL SEEDS

Though never asking for referrals is what makes my referral generating system different from others, the secret sauce to making referrals happen is to weave in language that plants referral seeds. A referral seed is language you use to "plant" the idea of referrals in the mind of your referral source or those you want to become a referral source. The use of the referral seeds in combination with the memorable and meaningful touch points allows you to be remembered on a different level while suggesting a future action for the referral source. Another title for this chapter could have been "What to Do Instead of Asking."

While using the right kind of referral seed allows you to never need to ask for a referral, you do need to know the key moments to use the right language, to plant those referral seeds. You learned a little about planting a referral seed in Chapter 9 when I provided the language to use when writing a thank-you note for a referral received. But in this chapter, we will dive in deeper.

There are many opportunities to plant referral seeds, and to plant them correctly you need to know when those moments occur and what language to use. Now remember, these moments are not opportunities for you to leverage or manipulate your referral source or soon-to-be referral source. The language must be genuine and truthful for

YOU DO NEED TO KNOW THE KEY MOMENTS TO USE THE RIGHT LANGUAGE, TO PLANT THOSE REFERRAL SEEDS.

it to work. Most people can tell when someone is being fake. Here are some of those key moments to use the right language to plant referral seeds (not an exhaustive list):

- what you say in a thank-you card
- what you say when someone asks, how is business?
- the message you include with your touch points
- how you invite referral sources to an event that is not just for referral sources
- what you say when you forgot to thank someone
- what to say when you have been referred a family member
- what to say to someone who is not yet referring people to you
- how to turn a warm lead into a referral

- how to turn an introduction into a referral
- how to turn word-of-mouth buzz into a referral
- what you say during your first meeting with the prospect who was referred to you and is considering working with you

These are all moments to show our gratitude and authenticity to our referral sources and those being referred to us, but also to weave in the right language, to plant referral seeds. Remember, this language is never manipulative, never takes advantage of the referral source and is true to who we are and how we feel about our referral sources.

DISCOVERING THE POWER OF REFERRAL SEEDS

Planting referral seeds is a little bit of an art form that can certainly be learned once you understand the key pieces or formula for every message. In working with the students in my Growth By Referrals program, I have had the opportunity to provide language for many different scenarios, and I have found that providing feedback on language allows my students to become confident about creating their own language when they follow the referral seed language formula. I believe the immediate, hands-on support I provide allows my students to show up in the right way for their referral sources so they don't miss an opportunity to plant a seed.

To be honest, this is something I discovered by accident a few years ago. In creating all the parts of the process that would eventually become my Growth By Referrals system, I would test ideas just to see what would happen. Now remember, my goal for my referral system was to continually create a steady stream of prospective new clients to my coaching practice so I wouldn't suffer another business failure. I needed to keep the pipeline full of potential new prospects. One year I decided to write a thank-you card at the end of the year thanking my referral sources for the referrals they sent to me that year. On a whim, I included the name of the person that particular referral source had referred to me. (Yes, I had the names handy because I track all referrals, even those that do not become clients).

What I realized is that what I did—by including the names of the people that person had referred to me—was connect on a different level. I was showing my referral source that not only did I appreciate the referral, but it meant enough to me to remember exactly who they had referred to me. This particular thank-you note was sent at the end of the year, which means if they had referred me at the beginning of the year or even three of four months earlier, I showed them by my actions that their referral was worthy of not only an immediate thank-you note (which I sent when the referral was received), but also was worthy of another note at the end of the year.

The idea of using the person's name that was referred to you (the prospective new client) is planting a referral seed. As you learned in Chapter 9, you do this in the immediate thank-you card, **but that is not the only time**.

It was including the name in an end-of-year card—plus additional language—that translated to my receiving new referrals I had not experienced before. Anyone can write a note thanking someone for their generosity; but letting them know I remembered all the times they referred someone to me served to strengthen our relationship. They weren't expecting it, and I was able to be memorable and meaningful, separating myself from anyone else they may have referred people to. What I found was this also created an uptick in referrals at the beginning of the next year since I sent these out at the end of the year, which was an unexpected bonus. That is when I realized how powerful referral seeds can be, that there is a formula to follow and all the many opportunities to plant them with our referral sources or soon-to-be referral sources.

Word of caution, just as your referral generating plan (see Chapter 10) cannot produce the results you want without using the right language, just using the language in only one scenario (like the thank-you card) or sporadically won't provide you the results you want. The referral generating plan allows you to nurture your referral sources, and the referral seed language allows you to connect and build the habit of referring. These two components build off of each other and using them together is the best way to have referral success.

But this chapter is about the language, so let's look at how and when you plant referral seeds. In particular, let's look at three ways to plant seeds that are easy to follow; you can also put them into action immediately. Make sure to review the list of some of those key moments I listed at the beginning of the chapter to understand the myriad opportunities to plant referral seeds.

THREE REFERRAL SEEDS TO MASTER

Here are three immediate application times, fairly common situations, in which you can plant a referral seed.

1. In conversation with a client, a COI or someone in your network
2. When someone is considering hiring you
3. When you start working with a new client (this is *not* what you think)

Let's look at each one in more detail so you can extract what to do and apply it (preferably today!).

1. IN CONVERSATION WITH SOMEONE IN YOUR NETWORK, A CLIENT OR COI

The goal is to correctly answer the "how's business?" question. How many times a day are you asked, "How's business?" when you run into or have a meeting with a friend, colleague, client, associate, or just about anyone in your network? Just think back to the last networking event you attended. How many times did you answer the "How's business?" or "How are things going?" questions?

The "How's business?" question is asked a lot because it is an easy conversation starter. Asking it is great but I am more interested in *how you answer it*. I'll bet you say "busy" or "good" or maybe in some cases if you are being really honest, "things have been better."

On the surface nothing seems to be wrong with these answers, but they do nothing for you, particularly when you say "busy" or "good." Why? The "busy" and "good" responses aren't memorable. They mean nothing. They are quickly forgotten. And they don't keep the conversation going. Your aim should be to answer in a way that keeps the conversation going. So the next time you are asked "How's business?" what I want you to say is this…

> *Business is growing. I can't believe how many referrals I've recently received.*

Or

> *Thanks for asking. I'm excited that two new clients I just started working with came through referrals.*

Or something like this…

> *Business is growing like crazy. When I look at my client base I'm astounded how many of my clients were referred to me. That lets me know I'm doing something right."*

Now you may have to tweak this language to work for you and to accurately reflect your business and actual referral count because you can't be authentic if you are lying. But never miss an opportunity to plant a seed that your business is growing due to referrals. Also, your answer doesn't need a lot of explaining, so you can give your answer and then be quiet to see if it triggered interest and they want to know more. Your answer will be memorable by itself no matter what response you are able to give about your referral success, no matter how small or large.

Planting a seed like this allows you the opportunity to remind people that your work is:

- Amazing enough to receive referrals
- That you value and appreciate receiving referrals
- You are working to grow a referral-based business

But your answer does one more important thing for the person receiving the answer. Your answer is a pattern interrupt, which is defined as something not expected or goes against the automatic answer someone is subconsciously waiting for. A pattern interrupt will stop the person and get their attention. It is when you have their attention that the referral seed is actually planted. In fact, it might even lead to a better conversation about business. Having someone engage in conversation with you about referrals is a great way to make sure they understand the business you are in, the type of clients you work with (particularly who your ideal client is) and could lead them to ask you about what is it that you do that generates so many referrals.

When a potential new COI recognizes that other people are referring you, you gain instant credibility or social proof. This is a crucial step in nurturing potential referrals and turning this person into a referral source who refers you again and again.

Word of caution: If the conversation gets going around your business and referrals, absolutely make sure you leave time during the conversation for you to ask about them, their business and show genuine interest in how they are doing. This builds the foundation of a two-way relationship. Referral sources will refer you because someone they know needs you, but knowing you care about them—not just the referral they sent to you—is key to strengthening the relationship.

One way to show a genuine interest in helping their business is to ask them what an ideal client looks like for them; then you can always be on the lookout for those who would be make a good referral for them. Referrals should never be a "tit for tat" (meaning I give so you must give), but being able to refer back and forth is a great outcome.

Now some will ask if using this type of language to answer the question "How's business" will come across as bragging. Because your answer is a pattern interrupt and you are not having this same conversation with the same person day in and day out, it won't usually come across as bragging; nevertheless, you know who you are talking to (if they aren't new) so use your best judgment. But you should be willing to try this before you starting deciding when to use the language and when to not use the language.

Answering the "How's business?" question allows you to plant seeds, seeds that with proper care and cultivation will grow into referrals. Not every seed, of course, but continued and wide spread use of planting this particular seed will bear fruit and grow many people who know you work from referrals.

2. WHEN SOMEONE IS CONSIDERING WORKING WITH YOU

When your potential and current clients understand from the beginning that you work from referrals, it becomes ingrained in them. Like a way they just think of you. They associate you with having clients who come through referrals. Now, your prospects and clients won't immediately think of you in this way, so you need to plant this truth early and often if you can. That is more limited with prospects, but it's still worth knowing the language to use because if they do become a client they will have already linked referrals and you together. Remember, the goal is to be professional and to use the language with great ease. It can't be forced and it can't feel inauthentic.

I loved an email I received from one of my students in the Growth By Referrals online program. Her name is Kathleen, and she shared that right after buying my program she just happened to mention to someone in conversation that she has bought my program to learn more about generating referrals; that person later sent her two referrals. That shows the power of planting a seed to generate referrals. I believe this early planting worked because Kathleen was genuine in telling this person about it. It just came up in conversation and Kathleen showed enthusiasm about it. It had what seems to be an unintended positive effect because it was authentic and professional. But what it really did was allow Kathleen to plant the seed. This is one example of the importance of planting the referral seeds early.

When someone is considering hiring you they are in a phase referred to as the buyer's journey. The buyer's journey is defined as the process a prospective client goes through when they are making the decision to work with you. It starts from the moment they connect the dots that they have a problem in their business or life that someone can solve through a product or service. It ends when they decide who they will hire or buy from—preferably you, of course. The buyer's journey ends when they decide to hire you or not hire you.

During the buyer's journey don't miss an opportunity to let them know how many of your clients come to you through referrals. I never shy away from telling someone that 90 to 95 percent of my clients come through referrals but I'm strategic about when I share it. I never force it into the conversation. If your percentage isn't a number that is impressive to you then you can say how many of your most recent clients were referred to you. This is typically woven into the conversation when they ask you about your business, how you got started, what it looks like to work with you, or what your costs are. At some point during one of those questions you need to be able to weave in the referral language.

Keep in mind, planting the seed early with a prospect who may become a client allows them to associate you with referrals right from the start.

3. DURING THE NEW CLIENT EXPERIENCE

The new client experience picks up where the buyer's journey ends and is the early process of touch points a new client goes through when they first start working with you. It starts when they say yes to working with you and typically includes the first few weeks or month of being a new client. The "new" period or stage ends as they continue to engage with you as the real work begins. After the new stage, they move into the active or ongoing client experience stage.

When a client starts working with me I try to always make the connection early to remind them of how they found me. Which means I will remind them during our first session together that they were referred to me, and I always remind them of who referred them to me. When they can connect our working together not just because they were referred but also to the person who made the referral happen, it allows the idea of referrals to stick better. I usually just mention that I'm grateful "Jane Doe" referred them to me so that we have the opportunity to work together. That's it. Nothing dramatic or drawn out, just a seed planted.

You can also apply this same concept during the buyer's journey as well. If the prospect you are meeting with was connected to you via a referral, then by all means remind them during your meeting, and use the name of the person who referred them to you.

***

Remember, we are building relationships, so our outreach, our touch points, must be different from our marketing or prospecting tactics. Even though we are not asking for referrals, we are being strategic. We are doing something to generate referrals; it just happens to not include a direct ask for referrals—ever. There are many things we do for someone to encourage referrals—in between actually receiving them. After all we are developing a relationship to nurture ongoing referrals. But the three tips in this chapter

> WE ARE BUILDING RELATIONSHIPS, SO OUR OUTREACH, OUR TOUCH POINTS, MUST BE DIFFERENT FROM OUR MARKETING OR PROSPECTING TACTICS

provide you with immediate action steps to take prior to having the system in place.

The system—the referral generating plan—I teach inside my Growth By Referrals program builds on planting the right referral seeds for the long term so you can cultivate ongoing referrals and be authentic in the process. But a process you don't execute on really doesn't do you any good; it's the final step in the five steps of creating a referral generating plan that allows us to make the process manageable.

Chapter Twelve

STEP FIVE:
AUTOMATE THE PLAN
AND MEASURE RESULTS

If Step Three, creating the referral generating plan, is the *what you do,* then this step—Step Five is *how you make it happen.* Step Five is the execution of the plan and, of course, tracking and measuring what is working and what is not working. The automation portion of this plan is really based on the scheduling of your touch points. You cannot automate or outsource all of the pieces. You will have some work to do. For example, you will need to write your thank-you notes. And I can hear some of you know groaning about how bad your handwriting is. That doesn't matter; just write slowly and the best you can. You must show up authentically for this to work.

The template I use to build my Growth By Referrals VIP and online students' plans allows us to easily translate the material into our current calendar (I use Outlook, but Google and other calendars work as well) or a project management system if you have one. Keep in mind, it is more difficult to program the plan into your CRM tool since you would have to add the follow-up activities for each person individually. Also, you definitely don't need a project

YOU MUST SHOW UP AUTHENTICALLY FOR THIS TO WORK

management system. You just need a way to calendar out what you are going to do so you actually do it when the time comes.

Once we have the plan built and set to be executed, we need to track and measure our results. If we don't track a few key metrics, then we won't know what is working and what is not working. Here are the few key metrics to track:

- Number of referrals received by year (and you can break down by month as well as track trends over time)
- Number of referrals received from each referral source (Someone who sent you ten referrals in a year needs an upgraded outreach or touch point experience more than someone who sent you one or two referrals a year.)
- Increase in number of referrals received from individual referral sources year after year (What we want to know is if they sending you more referrals in a year now that you are following the plan.)
- Breakdown of referrals received by type of referral sources (client or COIs)

- Your close rate for each individual referral source (meaning the average number or percent you close from individual sources) helps you understand who is setting you up correctly and who is not.

***

Well, there you have it. The Five Steps to Creating a Referral Generating Plan. Carve out time today or at least this week to understand all five steps and start applying what you learned in your business. I encourage you download the Five Steps to a Referral Generating Plan Cheat Sheet you can find in the chapter resource section found at www.generatingbusinessreferrals.com/resources. Download this cheat sheet so you have an easy-to-reference guide to each of the five steps.

While it may sound like a lot of work, my referral generating plan is the easiest process I follow in my business, it produces the greatest results. I love that it is simple and authentic. It is because of its simplicity and authenticity that I am willing to follow it, year after year after year.

<u>Chapter Download:</u>
5 Steps to Creating a Referral Generating Plan
To download please visit:
www.generatingbusinessreferrals.com/resources

Final Thoughts

Please close your eyes (okay, just close one until you read the next line). Imagine what the perfect day looks like for you and your business. Just take a moment, close your eyes, and imagine it. It's okay, I'll wait.

What did you imagine?

For me the perfect day involves getting a walk in, eating breakfast and dinner with my husband and kids, spending time working on my most valuable and important tasks (like creating content, delivering a VIP session or corporate workshop, or answering questions from my online community*) AND finding a referral or two arrived in my email inbox.

Do you know what my perfect day says to me? It says I took time to take care of myself, I took time to invest in my family, I took time to provide value to my clients and online community, and I received a reminder of what great work I do because someone referred a new client to me.

My perfect day says something else to me too. It says that my business grew, and I didn't have to stress about where the next client was coming from. It means I can relax and focus on doing great work instead of worrying about being a great "salesperson," which I did not go into business to become. Quite the contrary, I started my business because I enjoy making a difference for my clients and delivering a service they need. My perfect day is now a reality—not every day—but close.

What did you imagine? What does your perfect day say to you? Is your business growing with less effort because you receive more referrals than you could possibly handle? Are you able to spend time working on what matters most—the value you bring to your clients instead of hustling for the next client? Did you imagine spending time taking care of your referral sources by showing them the gratitude they deserve, continually strengthening your relationship with them and honoring the commitment you made to be meaningful and memorable so you stay top of mind? Did you imagine this new reality as your new normal, the perfect day or week imagined as a real day?

It is possible. Though not without some work and willingness to shift your mindset. Remember, referrals never show up if you aren't referable, if you don't provide value, if you don't do great work, if you aren't memorable and meaningful, if you don't stay top of mind, and if you don't plant referral seeds. And they definitely won't show up if you are constantly asking for them either. Your referrals also won't show up if you do nothing at all.

You can have referrals without asking. You have already taken the first step. You picked up this book to learn how to generate referrals without asking for them. Now you just need to take the next step. Download the resources provided to you in the chapters at www.generatingbusinessreferrals.com/resources and start applying what you learned. If you want to go further, then check out the ways to work with me at the back of this book or at www.growthbyreferrals.com. I look forward to you finally experiencing the referral experience you deserve.

It's time to take control of your referrals. Don't delay!

Stacey

Join the online community of other business professionals who believe you can generate referrals without asking. Join us in the free Referrals Without Asking Facebook group at www.facebook.com/groups/referralswithoutasking

Work With Me

CUSTOM-BUILT
REFERRAL PLAN

Your year-long Referral Generating Plan is built customized for you including an action plan so all you have to do is execute.

- Includes the touch points, the language and messaging, timeline and execution plan.
- Reminders are sent in advance of each touch point
- Quarterly check-ins on progress and results tracking
- Access to me for one full year of implementation
- Access to Growth By Referrals online program
- Invitation to join the paid, student-only Facebook group for ongoing support

(From start to finish, it takes on average 30 days to deliver your custom-built referral plan.)

VIP REFERRAL BUILDING SESSION

Together, we build your Referral Generating Plan during our 4 hour session held in Charlotte or virtually over Zoom.

- Includes the touch points, the language and messaging, timeline and execution plan
- 30-day check in call
- Access to me for one full year of implementation
- Access to Growth By Referrals online program
- Invitation to join the paid, student-only Facebook group for ongoing support

GROWTH BY REFERRALS
PROGRAM

Looking for a Do-It-Yourself option? Join the Growth By Referrals online program. The entire Referral Generating Plan is available through six video modules walking you, by the hand, through each step in the process including resources, handouts and support.

- Unlimited and lifetime access to the program to go back and review whatever you need.
- Go as fast or slow as you want…even in your pjs on your front porch.
- When you complete all six modules you will have built your year-long referral generating plan and be ready to execute.
- All future program upgrades are included for free
- Invitation to join the paid, student-only Facebook group for ongoing support

Find out more at www.GrowthByReferrals.com

About the Author

Photo Credit: @treffeisenmedia

With one business failure under her belt, Stacey Brown Randall knew when she started business #2 she had better do things different or she'd end up working for Corporate America for the rest of her life. That wasn't an option she was willing to accept.

So, with the launch of business #2, she cracked the code on how to generate referrals without asking. In her first year as a business coach she hit 112 referrals and continues to generate triple digit referrals every year since. Now she has helped hundreds build their own referral generating plans and has been featured on numerous radio and podcast shows including Real

Estate Rockstar Radio, Nice Guys on Business, Voice America Business and WHNZ Tampa Bay.

Stacey lives in Charlotte, NC with her husband and three kids.

Bibliography

1. Covey, Stephen M. R. *The Speed of Trust.* New York: Simon & Schuster, 2008.
2. Nielsen Corporation. "Digital Formats Are Among The Most Trusted Advertising Sources Despite Slow Growth." Nielsen.com. http://www.nielsen.com/us/en/insights/news/2015/digital-formats-are-among-the-most-trusted-advertising-sources-despite-slow-growth.html (accessed August 28, 2016).
3. Shah, Parthiv. *Business Kamasutra, From Persuasion to Pleasure.* California: Motivational Press, 2016.
4. Wagner, Eric. "Five Reasons 8 Out of 10 Businesses Fail." Forbes.com. https://www.forbes.com/sites/ericwagner/2013/09/12/five-reasons-8-out-of-10-businesses-fail/#6517a26c6978 (accessed June 27, 2017).

Morgan James
Speakers Group

We connect Morgan James published
authors with live and online events
and audiences who will benefit
from their expertise.

Morgan James makes all of our titles available
through the Library for All Charity Organization.

www.LibraryForAll.org

Printed in the USA
CPSIA information can be obtained
at www.ICGtesting.com
JSHW082345140824
68134JS00020B/1889

9 781683 509264